Cambridge Opera Handbooks

W. A. Mozart
Così fan tutte

Published titles

Alban Berg: *Lulu* by Douglas Jarman
Alban Berg: *Wozzeck* by Douglas Jarman
Hector Berlioz: *Les Troyens* by Ian Kemp
Georges Bizet: *Carmen* by Susan McClary
Benjamin Britten: *Billy Budd* by Mervyn Cooke and Philip Reed
Benjamin Britten: *Death in Venice* by Donald Mitchell
Benjamin Britten: *Peter Grimes* by Philip Brett
Benjamin Britten: *The Turn of the Screw* by Patricia Howard
Claude Debussy: *Pelléas et Mélisande* by Roger Nichols and Richard Langham Smith
C. W. von Gluck: *Orfeo* by Patricia Howard
Leoš Janáček: *Kát'a Kabanová* by John Tyrrell
Claudio Monteverdi: *Orfeo* by John Whenham
W. A. Mozart: *La clemenza di Tito* by John Rice
W. A. Mozart: *Così fan tutte* by Bruce Alan Brown
W. A. Mozart: *Don Giovanni* by Julian Rushton
W. A. Mozart: *Die Entführung aus dem Serail* by Thomas Bauman
W. A. Mozart: *Idomeneo* by Julian Rushton
W. A. Mozart: *Le nozze di Figaro* by Tim Carter
W. A. Mozart: *Die Zauberflöte* by Peter Branscombe
Giacomo Puccini: *La Bohème* by Arthur Groos and Roger Parker
Giacomo Puccini: *Tosca* by Mosco Carner
Richard Strauss: *Arabella* by Kenneth Birkin
Richard Strauss: *Elektra* by Derrick Puffett
Richard Strauss: *Der Rosenkavalier* by Alan Jefferson
Richard Strauss: *Salome* by Derrick Puffett
Igor Stravinsky: *The Rake's Progress* by Paul Griffiths
Giuseppe Verdi: *Falstaff* by James A. Hepokoski
Giuseppe Verdi: *Otello* by James A. Hepokoski
Richard Wagner: *Die Meistersinger von Nürnberg* by John Warrack
Richard Wagner: *Parsifal* by Lucy Beckett
Kurt Weill: *The Threepenny Opera* by Stephen Hinton

W. A. Mozart
Così fan tutte

BRUCE ALAN BROWN
University of Southern California

CAMBRIDGE
UNIVERSITY PRESS

Published by the Press Syndicate of the University of Cambridge
The Pitt Building, Trumpington Street, Cambridge CB2 1RP
40 West 20th Street, New York, NY 10011–4211, USA
10 Stamford Road, Oakleigh, Melbourne 3166, Australia

© Cambridge University Press 1995

First published 1995

Printed in Great Britain at Woolnough Bookbinders Ltd,
Irthlingborough, Northants.

A catalogue record for this book is available from the British Library

Library of Congress cataloguing in publication data
Brown, Bruce Alan.
    W. A. Mozart, Così fan tutte / Bruce Alan Brown.
        p.   cm. – (Cambridge opera handbooks)
    Includes bibliographical references and index.
    ISBN 0 521 43134 4 (hardback) – ISBN 0 521 43735 0 (paperback).
    1. Mozart, Wolfgang Amadeus, 1756–1791. Così fan tutte.
I. Title. II. Series.
ML410.M9B819 1996
782. 1–dc20   95–9885 CIP MN

ISBN 0 521 43134 4 hardback
ISBN 0 521 43735 0 paperback

For my mother
Margaret Ufford Brown –

'Femmina. . .senza paraggio'

Contents

Illustrations

General preface

This is a series of studies of individual operas, written for the serious opera-goer or record-collector as well as the student or scholar. Each volume has three main concerns. The first is historical: to describe the genesis of the work, its sources or its relation to literary prototypes, the collaboration between librettist and composer, and the first performance and subsequent stage history. The history is itself a record of changing attitudes towards the work, and an index of general changes of taste. The second is analytical and it is grounded in a very full synopsis which considers the opera as a structure of musical and dramatic effects. In most volumes there is also a musical analysis of a section of the score, showing how the music serves or makes the drama. The analysis, like the history, naturally raises questions of interpretation, and the third concern of each volume is to show how critical writing about an opera, like production and performance, can direct or distort appreciation of its structural elements. Some conflict of interpretation is an inevitable part of this account; editors of the handbooks reflect this – by citing classic statements, by commissioning new essays, by taking up their own critical position. A final section gives a select bibliography and guide to other sources.

Acknowledgements

Of the many debts of gratitude incurred in the preparation of this study, the most profound are owed to Daniel Heartz and Michel Noiray, for their many insightful comments and helpful corrections. I am grateful also to Dexter Edge, Dorothea Link, and in particular to Elizabeth Dunstan, for generously making available to me material not yet published. I have benefited significantly from John A. Rice's intimate knowledge of the Viennese Burgtheater during this period; he graciously and immediately shared with me his discovery of important material regarding *Così fan tutte* and Salieri. My thinking on the opera has been greatly enriched also by the ideas of Mary Hunter, Louise Geist, Ronald J. Rabin, Edmund Goehring and Alessandro Di Profio. My gratitude extends also to Penny Souster and Victoria Cooper at Cambridge University Press for their encouragement, and even more for their patience; and to reader Michael Black for his felicitous queries and suggestions. Finally, I thank the University of Southern California for granting a semester's sabbatical leave which I used in furtherance of this project.

The illustrations in this book appear by kind permission of the following: Plates 1 and 2, Bildarchiv der Österreichischen Nationalbibliothek, Vienna; Plate 3, Deutsches Theatermuseum, Munich; Plate 4, Doheny Memorial Library, University of Southern California, Los Angeles; Plate 5, Glyndebourne Festival Opera; Plate 6, Peter Krupenye; Plate 7, Christer Ulvås; Plate 8, Marie-Noëlle Robert.

1 *Introduction*

Towards the end of December 1789 Mozart sent a note to his friend, creditor and fellow Freemason, Michael Puchberg, inviting him to a private rehearsal of a new opera he had written for Vienna's court theatre:

> Next month I will receive from the directorate (according to the current arrangement) 200 ducats for my opera; if you can and will lend me 400 florins until then, you will lift your friend from the greatest embarrassment, and I give you my word of honour that you will have the money back at the appointed time in cash and in full, with all my thanks. . . [After cancelling an engagement for the next day:] But I invite you (and you alone) to my apartment at 10 in the morning on Thursday [the 31st] for a little opera rehearsal – I'm inviting only you and Haydn. . .[1]

One reason for this invitation (as also a later one, to the first orchestral rehearsal) was to impress Puchberg that Mozart was in fact producing works that would bring in money with which to repay him for past and future loans. But the presence of Haydn, whose opinion Mozart respected greatly, is an indication of the composer's pride in his new opera, *Così fan tutte*, and that musical enjoyment was the main reason for the invitation. Mozart's stance towards the work – the last of three operas created in collaboration with Lorenzo Da Ponte – is a matter of some importance, as several early critics attempted to distance the composer from his librettist's text, in order to remove what they considered to be a blot on his reputation. Already in 1791 a correspondent for the *Annalen des Theaters*, reporting on a performance in Frankfurt, called the opera 'a miserable Italian product with the powerful, sublime music of a Mozart'.[2] The Bohemian Franz Xaver Němetschek (Niemetschek), otherwise one of Mozart's warmest supporters, wondered how the composer could 'waste his heavenly sweet melodies on such a miserable and clumsy text'.[3] And somewhat later, the Russian critic Aleksandr Ulybyshev wrote of Mozart having faced the dilemma

1

of having either to set an 'uncomposable' text, or consciously to ignore much of what Da Ponte had created.[4]

From a modern perspective, such views hardly seem comprehensible, for *Così fan tutte* is now generally acknowledged to be a masterpiece of comic invention, in which disturbing psychological issues are probed at least as deeply as in the prior collaborations of its authors. Some basic facts about the opera can be singled out as contributing to the puzzlement of some spectators and critics. The supposed lack of a model text has left Da Ponte more vulnerable to criticism than in the cases of his Beaumarchais-derived *Figaro*, and of *Don Giovanni*, which was based on a libretto by Bertati, and a long theatrical tradition before that. More so than those works, *Così* also demands a listener well versed in the history of operatic conventions, and with a fine sensitivity to irony. Most crucially, the 'philosophy' voiced in *Così* belongs to a world-view that was already on the wane when the opera was new. As both Daniel Heartz and Andrew Steptoe have suggested, the fine shades of distinction in *Così* between various types or stages of romantic involvement, and the elaborate pairings and repairings of the four lovers are much as one finds in the plays and novels of Marivaux, in the first half of the century.[5] One might also draw an analogy to the painter Fragonard, whose art encompasses far more than the rococo frivolity critics have mostly seen in it, and whose reputation is only now undergoing a thorough rehabilitation.

Attempts such as Da Ponte's to reconcile love with reason lost much of their credibility in the nineteenth century, which ushered in more rigid views of bourgeois morality and new constructions of sexual roles. The mockery in *Così* of fidelity in love, by the philosophical Alfonso and the worldly-wise Despina, was not likely to encounter open sympathy in the Vienna of Joseph II's successors, at a time when personal and political freedoms were coming to be equated with radical notions emanating from Revolutionary France. *Così fan tutte* is comparable to *Die Zauberflöte*, in that both are statements of allegiance to a world-order under attack. Both operas' librettists firmly place their faith in 'reason': Da Ponte in the motto of his final chorus, Schikaneder in allusions to the tenets of Freemasonry, whose adherents were then being persecuted in Vienna. In this respect, a 1791 pamphlet entitled *Anti-da Ponte* is revealing in its ridicule of Da Ponte for clinging to the memory of the dead Emperor Joseph in an attempt to retain his own position as theatre-poet.

Even after the plot of *Così* had lost some of its shock value, spectators were hard pressed to fit the opera into a Mozart canon that emphasized the imposing and the tragic: the late symphonies, the minor-mode piano concertos, *Don Giovanni* and *Die Zauberflöte*. At the start of the twentieth century, *Così fan tutte* was revived as something of a connoisseur's opera – indeed, the nature of Da Ponte's text gives much basis for such a view. But it was principally the music, and not the plot, that was that the object of revival and of critical attention. The same Edward Dent who called *Così*'s libretto 'as perfect. . .as any composer could desire' nevertheless declared that in the dénouement it made no difference at all '[w]hether the ladies pair off with their original lovers or their new ones'.[6] Not until 1954 was any serious attempt made to come to grips with the basic material of the plot and its sources.[7] The discovery that these lay in Greek myths and Italian literary classics has done much to stimulate further research on its text, as well as more thoughtful productions of the opera.

'. . .dramma che tiene il terzo loco. . .'

Così fan tutte is more intimately bound up with the other two products of Mozart's collaboration with Da Ponte than is often realized. The librettist's own characterization of *Così* in his memoirs as a 'drama which holds third place among the sisters born of that most celebrated father of harmony' (Mozart) clearly links it with these other works.[8] But this formulation also seems evasive, even deprecating; for Da Ponte, the work's title was not even *Così fan tutte*, but rather *La scuola* [or *scola*] *degli amanti*. There was good reason for this circumspection: Da Ponte intended his memoirs for a public consisting primarily of his own female students of Italian, who no doubt would be scandalized by a phrase such as 'così fan tutte', and by any explanation of its premise.[9] But to a Viennese public that knew both titles, the first of them would immediately have called to mind a phrase sung by Basilio in *Le nozze di Figaro*. As Count Almaviva discovers Cherubino hiding in a chair in Susanna's room, the cynical music master observes: 'Così fan tutte le belle, / Non c'è alcuna novità' (All women do that; there's nothing new about it). Mozart drives home the connection by quoting Basilio's musical motif in the first theme of the Presto section of *Così*'s overture (see Examples 1.1a–b):

4   *W. A. Mozart: Così fan tutte*

Example 1.1a

184

Basilio

Co - sì fan tut - te le bel - le;

non c'è al - cu - na no - vi - tà.

Example 1.1b

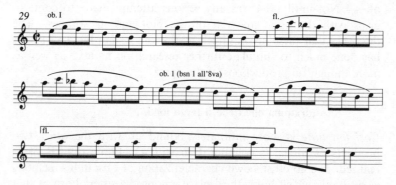

29 ob. I

fl.

ob. 1 (bsn 1 all'8va)

fl.

This trill-motif found its way also into the first finale of *Figaro*, where it is used to ironic effect: Susanna, having stepped out of her mistress's closet and confounded the count's suspicions concerning his wife and Cherubino, spurns his request to help calm her ire with the words 'Così si condanna chi può sospettar' (Thus is condemned one who is capable of suspicion).[10] Through this and further uses of the motif, it acquires the ability to communicate – and warn against – suspicion and jealousy. Thus its use in the overture of *Così* suggests that suspicion will figure prominently in the plot of this opera too. The motif's reappearance at the end of the third trio, just before the first change of scene, is doubly significant. As Ferrando and Guglielmo (abetted by Don Alfonso) confidently sing of the toasts they will make to Cupid once their wager is won and their women proven faithful, the whole orchestra takes up the trill, simultaneously depicting inebriation and mocking their certainty. By the time the officers actually do participate in a toast, in the second finale, they have lost their bet.

The theme of jealousy and its musical signifier were not the only means by which Mozart and his librettist encouraged spectators to associate *Così fan tutte* with *Le nozze di Figaro*. At several points they included textual or musical echoes of the earlier opera, clearly hoping to profit from its recent success with the Viennese public. The military chorus 'Bella vita militar', for example, returned to the spirit and subject matter of Figaro's aria 'Non più andrai, farfallone amoroso'. One prominently set text in *Così* amounted to an inversion of the sense of similar lines in *Figaro*. Susanna, while dressing up Cherubino in female garb as bait for the count (in No. 12 of the score), admires his youthful beauty, saying

> Se l'amano le femmine,
> Han certo il lor perchè.

(If women love him, they certainly have their reasons.).

Guglielmo, consoling the cuckolded Ferrando as best he can by saying that he is not alone in his predicament, ends his aria 'Donne mie, la fate a tanti' (No. 26) with a similarly worded couplet:

> Che se gridano gli amanti
> Hanno certo un gran perchè.

(For if lovers complain, they certainly have good reason.)

Guglielmo's aria is resonant also with Figaro's horn-accompanied warning to men concerning feminine cunning, 'Aprite un po' quegl'occhi' (likewise No. 26), and with other models to be discussed in Chapter 4.

In broader ways, too (traceable to a common origin in the *commedia dell'arte*), *Così fan tutte* clearly hearkens back to *Figaro* and to *Don Giovanni*. In the first place, all three operas are largely concerned with masks and disguises. In *Così* the officers' exotic garb gives them licence to indulge in amorous conduct not normally tolerated – with unintended consequences. Serenades are another feature common to the three Mozart/Da Ponte operas. These are used by the well-coached peasants in Act I of *Figaro*, by the *contadine* in Act III and by Susanna in the fourth-act garden scene of that opera, and by or for Don Giovanni at several points in the opera bearing his name. All these pieces, as well as Ferrando's promise of a serenade to his faithful beloved in No. 3 of *Così*, and the false Albanians' serenade in No. 21, reflect a general craze for such music among Viennese of the time.[11] Also not to be overlooked

among the threads linking the three operas are the complaints of
the servants Leporello and Despina (and Figaro's, of a quite different order), and the threatened swordplay between Alfonso and the
young officers at the beginning of *Così* – a comic echo of the fatal
duel at the start of *Don Giovanni*.

An alternative trilogy

The conspicuous lessons in relations between the sexes in these
operas moved Heartz to term them 'Three Schools for Lovers', after
Da Ponte's subtitle for *Così*. In each opera the men emerge
chastened; the same could be said of *Die Entführung aus dem Serail*,
on account of its second-act finale. (In *Così fan tutte* the women act
out with the 'Albanians' precisely what Belmonte and Pedrillo had
suspected their women of doing with the Turks.) But a slightly
different trio of operas given in Vienna might with equal logic be
termed 'Three Schools for Lovers': Paisiello's *Il barbiere di Siviglia*
(performed in 1783), *Le nozze di Figaro* and *Così fan tutte*. The first
two works, after plays by Beaumarchais, offer rather closer thematic
and musical parallels to *Così* than does *Don Giovanni*. The lessons
of the latter (Masetto's aside) are concerned with gross violations of
the social code, rather than the more delicate matter of trust. *Il
barbiere* and *Figaro*, on the other hand, quickly focus on the acute
psychological torment experienced by 'one capable of suspicion' (chi
può sospettar). 'Quelle rage a-t-on d'apprendre ce qu'on craint tou-
jours de savoir!' (What a fury one is in to find out what one always
fears to know!), Bartholo mutters to himself in Beaumarchais's
Barbier de Séville, as he furtively reads a letter he has snatched from
his young pupil Rosine. Paisiello and his librettist (usually said to
be Giuseppe Petrosellini) let this moment pass quickly in recitative,
but Da Ponte and Mozart seized upon the similarly disquieting lines
in the opening scene of *Le Mariage de Figaro*, and amplified them
in a musical number. In telling Figaro 'Discaccia i sospetti / Che
torto mi fan' (Chase away your suspicions which do me wrong), in
the duettino, No. 2, Susanna repeats 'sospetti' three times over,
which only augments his anxieties. It is just such torment that
Alfonso tells his friends not to go courting, in the opening scene of
Così. Echoing Susanna, the officers protest that Alfonso does their
women wrong ('. . .che torto le fa'); the difference is that in this
opera the women do give in.

Da Ponte's debt to the French dramatist extended also to matters
of technique. In *Le Barbier de Séville* Beaumarchais takes a fairly

common practice – the use of a play's title or subtitle within the text itself – and carries it to unprecedented lengths. The characters refer more than a dozen times to a fictitious *drame* called *La Précaution inutile*, which phrase Beaumarchais also used as the subtitle of his own comedy. The phrase is sometimes used complete (as at the end, where it is printed in italics), sometimes only allusively; in any case the repeated mentions of Bartholo's 'vain precautions' against seducers bring the audience into complicity with the playwright.[12] Da Ponte seems to have taken Beaumarchais's example as a challenge, for he too integrated his title – itself an explanation of why precautions are useless – into the architecture of his text. Just before the second finale Alfonso sings the motto 'Così fan tutte' didactically to his friends, who repeat it back to him. Mozart placed the same music near the beginning of the overture, expecting that auditors would recognize its significance. The critic Friedrich Rochlitz, writing in 1801, certainly did; he described the phrase as 'the signature of the whole, so plainly stated, as if it were piped from a tower. Can one mistake it? Could one do this any more beautifully?'[13] In addition to these two framing statements of the title, the one textless, the other verbatim, there are prominently placed versions which present it in different conjugations. At the end of her second-act aria Dorabella tells her sister to follow Cupid's dictates, 'che anch'io farò così' (for I shall do so too). A few scenes later Alfonso, too, hints at the motto, just before singing it, as he asks the men 'Ma l'altre, che faran, se ciò fer queste?' (But what will other women do, if these ones did this?). There is even what would appear to be a reference to the subtitle of *Il barbiere*. Concerning Despina's suggestion that they receive the two strangers, Dorabella asks her sister: 'Che imbroglio nascer deve / Con tanta precauzion?' (What trouble could arise, with so much precaution?) The opera's title, and the subtitle of Paisiello's opera before that, tell the audience that these precautions, too, will be useless.

It was natural enough that Da Ponte would imitate a prominent device from an opera that had been phenomenally popular with the Viennese public. But the Beaumarchais operas were neither the sole, nor even most important impulse behind the creation of *Così fan tutte* – whose text (as shall be seen) was offered initially to Salieri, not Mozart. Internal evidence points to a main source in one of the supreme landmarks of Italian literature – a body of work that Da Ponte spent much of his later career promoting, in England and America. What Da Ponte made of this source, and the degree to which Mozart's music seconded his intentions, will occupy us in several of the chapters to come.

2 Genesis

The mystery of the commission

There is little direct evidence on the origins of Mozart and Da Ponte's last operatic project. Mozart's correspondence is nearly silent on *Così fan tutte*, apart from two notes to Puchberg, cited above. This situation is in marked contrast to the case of *Idomeneo*, whose genesis is well documented because librettist and composer were working in different cities, and of *Die Entführung aus dem Serail*, on the progress of which Mozart reported enthusiastically to his father in Salzburg. Da Ponte's memoirs, written long after the fact, tell us little of substance about Così:

> . . .to my misfortune, there arrived [in Vienna] a singer, who without having any great claims to beauty, delighted me first of all by her voice; later, as she showed great propensity towards me, I ended by falling in love with her. . .For her I wrote *Il pastor fido* and *La cifra* with music by Salieri, two operas that marked no epoch in the annals of his musical glory, though they were in many parts very beautiful; and *La scola degli amanti*, with music by Mozart, a drama which holds third place among the sisters born of that most celebrated father of harmony.[1]

The singer in question was Adriana Ferrarese; Da Ponte's 'misfortune' was that she was already married (to one Luigi Del Bene), and that her offstage behaviour eventually caused both her and Da Ponte to be sacked. Ferrarese did not in any sense commission the operas Da Ponte mentions; the power to decide which operas were staged seems to have rested with the High Chamberlain, Count Franz Orsini-Rosenberg, and his assistants Baron Michael von Kienmayer and Johann Thorwart.[2] The correspondence between Joseph and Rosenberg makes no mention of *Così*, and this has left room for several rather fantastical accounts to arise as to how the opera came into being. One of these derives from Da Ponte himself. In the *Extract from the life of Lorenzo da Ponte*, a preliminary version of his memoirs that he wrote in 1819, the poet implies that

Mozart himself requested the libretto that became *Così*, specifically on account of the success of *Don Giovanni*:

"*Our opera of Don Giovanni,*" said he in a letter written to me from Prague, "*was represented last night to a most brilliant audience. . .The success of our piece was as complete as we could desire. Guardassoni* [the impresario] *came this morning almost enraptured with joy, into my room. Long live Mozart, long live Da Ponte, said he: as long as they shall exist, no manager shall know distress. Adieu! my dear friend. Prepare another opera for your friend Mozart.*" I was so happy of the opportunity, that although I had on hand at that time two other dramas, nevertheless I did not neglect my favourite Mozart, and in less than three months I gave a tragicomic drama, entitled Assur, king of Ormus, to Salieri. . .an heroicomic to Martini, called L'arbore di Diana, and a comic opera to Mozart, with the title of La scola degli Amanti, which was represented in Vienna, in Prague, in Dresden, and for several years in Paris, with unbounded applause. . .[3]

This letter from Mozart is generally regarded as a fabrication, and with good reason. For one thing, Da Ponte's *L'arbore di Diana* had preceded, not followed the opera for Prague, receiving its première on 1 October 1787. And in the complete Italian version of Da Ponte's memoirs, the trilogy is said to comprise *Axur, Don Giovanni*, and *L'arbore di Diana.*

1789 would seem far more likely than 1787 as a date of composition for the libretto of *Così fan tutte*, not least because the Viennese revival of *Le nozze di Figaro* in August of that year was just the sort of success which might lead to a new commission. The dire financial straits in which Mozart found himself by this time have led various writers to assume that Mozart had no choice but to set Da Ponte's 'unworthy' text to *Così*. Němetschek in 1797 stated that:

In the year 1789 in the month of December Mozart wrote the Italian comic opera *Così fan tutte*, or 'The School for Lovers'. . .It was not in his power to refuse the commission, and the text was given expressly to him.[4]

Georg Nikolaus von Nissen, the second husband of Constanze Mozart, plagiarized this passage in his biography of the composer,[5] and in 1837 the writer Friedrich Heinse sketched in some further details, claiming that

. . .Mozart was in fact expressly commissioned by Joseph II to compose this libretto. According to a rumour, an incident that had actually happened at that time in Vienna between two officers and their lovers, which was similar to the plot of the libretto, offered the emperor the occasion of honouring his court poet Guemara [*sic*; Heinse confuses Da Ponte with one of his successors, Giovanni de Gamerra] with the commission to make this piece of gossip into a *Drama giocoso da mettersi in musica.*[6]

As Kurt Kramer has pointed out, Joseph's declining health during this period makes it unlikely that he would have turned his attention to matters as frivolous as this. Since 1837, no firm evidence has come to light to substantiate Heinse's assertion.[7]

Another nearly contemporary explanation directly contradicts the notion of an imperial commission for *Così* going expressly to Mozart. During 1829 the British music publisher Vincent Novello and his wife Mary came to Salzburg in order to offer funds to Mozart's indigent sister, and while there also interviewed the composer's widow, Constanze Mozart Nissen. From her they heard that 'Salieri's enmity arose from Mozart's setting the *Così fan tutte* which he had originally commenced and given up as unworthy [of] musical invention.' The Italian had 'first tried to set this opera but failed, and the great success of Mozart in accomplishing what he could make nothing of is supposed to have excited his envy and hatred, and have been the first origin of his enmity and malice towards Mozart. . .'[8] Disregarding the fact that this was hardly the beginning of their rivalry, the scenario is chronologically plausible, as Salieri produced no other new opera between February and December of 1789. The story's fundamental truth can now be demonstrated, on account of John Rice's recent discovery, in the Music Collection of the Austrian National Library, of Salieri's autograph score for his settings of the first two numbers of the opera, catalogued (with their textual incipits) as 'Zwei Terzette'.[9] Though now reversed in order, in a modern binding, from the recitative text it is clear that 'È la fede delle femmine' was meant to follow 'La mia Dorabella capace non è', just as in Mozart's setting. 'È la fede' appears in full score, with much evidence of Salieri's revisions and corrections; for the other trio there are vocal parts only, apart from an initial orchestral flourish (itself much corrected), and the end of the number is not preserved. Evidently, the Metastasio-derived second trio (on which see below) was Salieri's initial point of attack – not surprisingly, in view of his literary interests, which Da Ponte thought highly unusual in a composer.[10]

The level of musical invention in Salieri's settings is consistent with abandonment of the project in the manner related by Mozart's widow. The finished piece, 'È la fede', moves amiably in 6/8 metre, with neither the mocking superiority of Mozart's Alfonso, nor the indignant explosions of the officers, as in the younger composer's setting (see Example 2.1).

In the sketched number there is even less, musically, to differentiate the characters – though the instruments presumably would have helped in this regard.

Although Constanze Mozart had reported that Salieri found the libretto 'unworthy [of] musical invention', Salieri's earlier willingness to set texts at least as risqué as that of *Così*, and on similar subject matter (notably Casti's *La grotta di Trofonio*) suggests that there were other factors in his decision not to perservere with his setting. One may well have been the souring of the composer's almost 'brotherly' friendship with Da Ponte, during Lent of 1789, as a result of the librettist's exclusion of Salieri's favourite, Catarina Cavalieri, from participation as a singer in the pasticcio *L'ape musicale*. Indeed, in listing the charges against his 'primary enemy' Salieri, in a later memorandum, Da Ponte mentions his having 'made sing in the capacity of prima donna la Cavalieri, whom I had proposed to pension'.[11]

Whether Mozart was the only other composer Da Ponte approached with his libretto, we cannot know. Given the success of his two prior collaborations with Da Ponte, he can hardly have hesitated to accept another libretto from him. In at least two respects it closely suited his tastes in opera buffa (as stated in a letter of 7 May 1783): in being newly written, as opposed to a revision of an earlier text, and in introducing 'two equally good female roles', one *seria*, and the other *mezzo carattere*.[12] But there can be little doubt that Mozart, in inheriting the project, demanded and got revisions from the poet – as is suggested by the quite different texts of the recitative that precedes 'È la fede', in his and Salieri's settings.[13] The changes here – which made for a much smoother, and more thoroughly comic introduction to the quotation from Metastasio – may be indicative of the two artists' negotiations generally.

The literary impulse

Though many critics have remarked on the density of literary allusion in *Così fan tutte*, few have realized that, rather than constituting a mere stylistic veneer, these are basic to the conception of the opera. In an important essay published in 1973, Kurt Kramer sought to explain Da Ponte's choice and treatment of subject matter largely in terms of his humanistic education, noting that the Latin and Italian poetic traditions provided a wealth of useful material on the theme of sexual jealousy.[14] Already in 1954 Ernst Gombrich had

Example 2.1

remarked on the striking parallels between *Così*'s plot and a Greek myth in which a husband tests the fidelity of his wife by courting her in disguise; Kramer went further, citing specific correspondences of language between *Così* and a less ancient version of the Procris story: the forty-third Canto of Ludovico Ariosto's epic *Orlando furioso*. That this sixteenth-century poem was indeed among the basic materials with which Da Ponte began his libretto is suggested also by the derivation of the names of all three of the opera's women from characters in *Orlando furioso*.[15] And in fact, as Elizabeth Dunstan has recently shown, Da Ponte drew not only on Canto 43, but also on Canto 24, and particularly Canto 28, with its multiple tests of fidelity. Most of the major themes of the opera can be found in *Orlando furioso*, as well as numerous locutions that audiences today know from recitatives and set pieces in *Così*.

That Da Ponte was prone to quotation and paraphrase is abundantly clear from his memoirs, which are peppered with Latin maxims, his own and others' verses, and praise for his nation's literary heritage. (Already in 1791, in the satirical pamphlet *Anti-da Ponte*, he was specifically charged with plundering the works of Metastasio and Beaumarchais, and mocked with various 'dapontisch' Latin or pseudo-Latin citations.) In *Così fan tutte*, Da Ponte's mouthpiece Alfonso uses a Latin phrase in his very first utterance, and starts the second number with a near-quotation of an entire quatrain from Metastasio.

Da Ponte's intention of creating a thoroughly allusive libretto is signalled by the opera's main title, a line from an ensemble in *Le nozze di Figaro*. But otherwise, the spectators were left to discover on their own the sources of the literary references. Da Ponte's reticence about his sources allowed for a promiscuous miscegenation of material from widely different periods, as well as for subtle manipulations and recombinations of elements from within Ariosto's epic. Spectators in the know could congratulate themselves on recognizing the familiar passages from Sannazaro and Metastasio, while savouring the comic distortions to which Ariostan characters and language were subjected. The number of persons capable of catching Da Ponte's allusions was probably not large. Though there was a substantial community of resident Italians and italophiles in Vienna at the end of the eighteenth century (when Lombardy, Tuscany and Trieste were all still Austrian possessions), only those who had received educations comparable to Da Ponte's, and who attended the opera, would have caught his allusions. One who probably did was Count János Fekete de Galántha, whose description of life in Josephinian Vienna includes remarks on the Italian opera repertory, and who even attempted a translation of *Orlando furioso* into his native Hungarian.[16]

Another person capable of appreciating the erudition in *Così* was Salieri, the composer who was originally to have composed the opera. In recounting the rupture in their friendship Da Ponte writes wistfully of having 'passed many learnedly happy hours' (. . .ore dottamente felici) in his company, which can hardly refer to any but literary diversions.[17] Any pleasure Salieri may have had in hearing the libretto in its musical dress must have been mixed with gall, given the circumstances.

Topicality

References to events, issues and persons of current interest to the original spectators are conspicuous in *Così fan tutte* – though scarcely more so than in *Figaro*, which brims with references to its own theatricality, or in *Don Giovanni*, the second finale of which includes a sustained joke about operas given recently in Prague and Vienna. But critics have been especially quick to note the topicality in *Così*, perhaps because of its central function in the work's first-act finale. The opera could readily accommodate topical references, given that its text was already saturated with literary allusions. Both devices shaped Da Ponte's libretto in ways more than incidental, lending an overt theatricality which participated significantly in the characterizations of the protagonists.

The extravagant Mesmerian charade in the first finale of *Così*, in which Despina magnetically cures the supposedly poisoned suitors, has been a major stumbling block for directors and spectators alike during much of the opera's history. In some nineteenth-century productions this action was eliminated, or replaced with a more logical ploy. But conversely, the modern director Jonathan Miller has staged the scene quite seriously, citing Mozart's childhood connection to the famous healer, who in 1768 (supposedly) sponsored a performance of Mozart's opera *Bastien und Bastienne* in the garden of his home in Vienna's Landstraße district.[18] The issue of the magnetic cure deserves to be considered seriously, as the episode is a turning point in the opera's plot. In considering the Mozarts' friendship with Franz Anton Mesmer, though, it would be a mistake to assume that either Leopold or (later) Wolfgang necessarily believed in the doctor's controversial theories. Self-interest was likely the most important factor: Mesmer had been willing to patronize the twelve-year-old prodigy, at a time when intrigues at court were preventing the performance of his opera *La finta semplice*. The Mozarts continued in later years to correspond with Mesmer and his cousin Joseph, but mainly about musical matters.[19] As for Da Ponte, it seems unlikely that he would have portrayed Mesmerism sympathetically in an opera that ended with the words 'Happy is he who. . .lets himself be guided by reason.' The historian Robert Darnton has described Mesmer's movement as specifically anti-Enlightenment in spirit, noting that his 'treatments' thrived in an atmosphere of 'overheated *sensiblerie*'; encouraged by appropriate music, subjects were induced to a state of crisis through manipulations of the 'magnetic fluid' passing through them.[20] When Mesmerism was officially debunked in 1784, by a French government commission that included Benjamin Franklin among its members, Mesmer's cures were attributed mainly to the suggestibility of his predominantly female subjects. The two sisters from Ferrara in *Così*, so susceptible to sentiment and sentimental language, would be willing believers in the veracity of the 'Albanian' suitors' Mesmerian paroxysms.

The music that accompanies Despina's ministrations, and especially the exaggerated cadential trills (bars 381 ff.) which poke fun at Mesmer's adopted home of France, dispel any thought that the collaborators meant the audience to take the action here at face value.[21] Yet, as Darnton reminds us, Mesmer's ideas were hardly more outlandish than Newton's 'invisible fluid', or Lavoisier's 'caloric'.[22] Even among the Viennese aristocracy there were followers of Mesmer – notably Count Franz Joseph von Thun, whose wife Wilhelmine was one of Mozart's most loyal patrons.[23]

For Viennese spectators at the first performances of *Così fan tutte*, war was a subject just as timely. Though the opera is set in Naples, and the nationality of the foe is never named, modern commentators have invariably connected this side of the plot to the war Emperor Joseph was then prosecuting against the Turks. The original audience probably did the same, given the charged atmosphere which followed the Austrians' capture of Belgrade in October of 1789. The Viennese press covered the military campaign almost to the exclusion of other news, and citizens and saw their city transformed by the increased military presence. The contemporary Viennese commentator Johann Pezzl referred to the war as a 'Schauspiel' (play) to which all Europe was a spectator;[24] how natural, then, to find reverberations of the Turkish war on the city's actual stages. Even in peacetime, military officers were a strong presence in the Viennese Burgtheater, renting places in the *parterre noble* – an enclosure directly in front of the orchestra and the stage; the playwright Joachim Perinet told how in this part of the auditorium one was wont to hear 'more talk of war than of theatre . . .'[25] Da Ponte and Mozart played directly to this segment of the public, beginning the very first scene of the opera with the loud boasts of the officers Guglielmo and Ferrando. The military side of the plot had its darker aspects, too: the dangers and hardships of war (described ironically by the chorus in No. 8), and the more ticklish issue of sexual constancy among soldiers (the subject of an entire aria, No. 12).

It seems obvious enough that the surname of Da Ponte's mistress Adriana Ferrarese, the first Fiordiligi, was what prompted the poet to specify that the two sisters came from Ferrara. That they are said to be 'living in Naples' is likely due to the famously intoxicating atmosphere of the port city, so conducive to love intrigues, and to the convenient proximity of Mount Vesuvius, already stereotypical in opera buffa as a metaphor for passion.[26] Da Ponte specifies a sea-side decoration twice during the opera, and astute stage designers would have needed little prompting to include recognizable Neapolitan features in the backdrops. We first meet the Ferrarese sisters in a 'giardino sulla spiaggia', as they gaze love-struck at portraits of their fiancés. By the end of this tableau, and the officers' feigned departure for battle, the setting itself is the subject of discourse, in the trio 'Soave sia il vento, / Tranquilla sia l'onda', No. 10. The invocation of the elements here encourages the abandoned women to indulge in their sorrow, and the spectators to forget that the poignant situation is the result of a bet. The second tableau of the next act brings back essentially the same set, now with *sedili d'erba* (turf benches), and a flower-bedecked barque full of musicians; in these exquisite surroundings the mysterious strangers begin seducing in earnest, with a serenade ('Secondate aurette amiche', No. 21) in which the elements are again addressed directly.

Da Ponte took care to integrate the opera's setting with the literary elements of the plot, in ways that were probably more obvious to eighteenth-century spectators than to us today. For those with some schooling in Italian letters, the conjunction in *Così* of 'Alfonso' and 'Ferrara', along with all the echoes of *Orlando furioso*, would have brought to mind the fact that the epic's author had worked in Ferrara at the court of Alfonso d'Este.[27] Da Ponte also gives Naples its due, referring to the city as 'Sebeto', a name dating back to Antiquity, in the early version of 'Rivolgete a lui lo sguardo'.[28] Da Ponte or Mozart apparently sensed that this last reference was too esoteric, for it was changed to 'Vienna' in Mozart's score. Mozart's decision to replace this piece was likely due to a number of factors, among which was a superabundance of other topical references: to the famous dancer Le Picq, to figures from mythology, even the furious Orlando himself.

But more pervasive in *Così* than any of these sorts of topicality are the many references to opera. These take both literary and musical form, implying a significant degree of coordination between poet and composer. In terms of function, the operatic quotations, clichés and parodies work like the literary allusions, affording the characters with ready-made substitutes for autonomous thinking when confronted with a situation. But whether invoked knowingly or unwittingly, the usual formulas do not always lead to the usual results, which makes for a vastly more interesting opera.

The compositional process

The decision to make opera a central topic in *Così fan tutte* naturally had consequences for the process by which the work took shape, particularly as regards its relationship to other operas recently produced in Vienna. But in what follows we will look at the opera's compositional history in the narrower sense, mainly as gathered from examination of the autograph score and other primary materials. Much of what follows is derived from the pioneering work of Alan Tyson, whose investigations of paper-types and watermarks have resulted in a greatly improved idea of Mozart's working methods.[29]

The August revival of *Le nozze di Figaro* was one of few bright spots for Mozart in 1789, during which he made a somewhat disappointing German concert tour, suffered both illness and the loss of a daughter at birth, and fell ever deeper into debt. In the new production of *Figaro*, the recently arrived Adriana Ferrarese took the role of Susanna, whose creator Nancy Storace meanwhile had returned to England. Not all of Storace's arias in *Figaro* suited Ferrarese, and Mozart's modifications and additions to her music helped to acquaint the composer with the voice and character of his future Fiordiligi. There is no mention of the new opera in Mozart's letters until the end of the year, when it was already in rehearsal. But it was probably underway by October, since the same paper-type on which he wrote most of the first act is used also in two insertion arias (K582 and 583) which he composed for Louise Villeneuve – Dorabella in *Così* – to use in a revival of Martín's *Il burbero di buon cuore*. The pieces were entered in Mozart's 'Verzeichnüß', or thematic catalogue, in October; performances of *Burbero* began on 9 November. Well before this date Da Ponte and Mozart were probably mapping out the general contours of their opera, perhaps even details as specific as aria- and verse-types. Mozart's work on *Così* seems to have been unusually rushed, to judge from the many abbreviations in his autograph score. Composition – though probably not orchestration – must have been largely complete by 31 December, the date of the 'small opera rehearsal' at his home to which Puchberg and Haydn were invited. Interestingly, in the same note he promises Puchberg that he will tell him about 'Salieri's cabals, which however have all come to naught' – a remark which resonates with the Novellos' comments quoted above. It was likewise in December that Mozart entered 'Rivolgete a lui lo sguardo' – or rather, 'à me' (No. 15a) – in his catalogue, as 'an aria which was meant for the opera *Così fan tutte*, for Benucci'. By this time, presumably, he had already composed the shorter and less risqué 'Non siate ritrosi' as its replacement.

For lack of other evidence, one is forced to fall back on the autograph score of *Così*, the first act of which was among the Mozart manuscripts considered lost after World War II, but which reappeared in the late 1970s at the Biblioteka Jagiellońska in Kraków, Poland. Paper-types are helpful in determining chronology mainly as regards Act I, for the second act was essentially all written on the same paper. Tyson discerned three layers in the composition of set pieces in Act I; simple recitatives would have been left until last. The earliest layer comprises numbers written exclusively on what he terms paper-type I: most of the ensembles (though not yet the finale), and a single aria, Dorabella's 'Smanie implacabili', No. 11. Though Mozart was familiar with the voices at his disposal, according to Tyson 'he may nevertheless have wished to complete the principal arias in consultation with the individual singers, at a time when most of the ensembles were behind him'.[30] Two numbers written on a mixture of paper-types I and II – Ferrando's 'Un'aura amorosa' (No. 17) and the ensemble 'Recitativo' 'Di scrivermi ogni giorno' – represent a later group, written as Mozart was exhausting his supply of type-I paper. Significantly, Mozart did not give it a separate number in his autograph score. His note 'ist ganz instrumentiert' was possibly intended for the court theatre's copyist, who might have thought that the sketchily scored piece was not yet finished. A third layer of pieces, all on type-II paper, includes Fiordiligi's showpiece 'Come scoglio' (No. 14); Despina's 'In uomini, in soldati' (No. 12); Guglielmo's 'Non siate ritrosi' (No. 15), which replaced the 'Rivolgete' aria; the first finale; and the easily dispatched Nos. 5 and 8 (Alfonso's 'Vorrei dir' and the chorus 'Bella vita militar' respectively). The overture was apparently composed last, as was Mozart's usual practice.

Tyson found additional clues on compositional chronology also in Mozart's inconsistency with regard to names. His crossing-out

and switching of the sisters' names on their staves in four of the
Act-I ensembles (all on type-I paper) in which they sing suggest that
in his haste to write out the score, Mozart initially confused the
ranges of the two singers. (There are similar changes as regards
Susanna and the Countess in the *Figaro* autograph.) In No. 10
(from Tyson's middle layer) and in the first finale, the women's
names are correctly entered. Also problematic was the name
Guglielmo – which in fact is never spelt that way either in Mozart's
score or in the original libretto. Using paper-types as an index,
Tyson distinguishes tentatively between early ('Guillelmo') and later
('Guilelmo') forms of the name, but draws no firm conclusions. One
might think that these variants represent a German-speaker's
difficulty with Italian liquid consonants, were it not for the fact that
Salieri's abortive score also unambiguously gives the reading
'Guilelmo'. This form persists in several early librettos and published
scores, only gradually giving way to the more common spelling
'Guglielmo'.

Several interesting *pentimenti* within the first act demonstrate
typically Mozartian refinements of dramaturgy. Early on, Mozart
extended No. 3 ('Una bella serenata') with a postlude on an extra
leaf of paper, thus rounding off the opera's opening trio of terzettos.
Revisions are also evident at the point where Despina is introduced.
Cancelled annotations in the score show that she was originally to
have had a cavatina at her entrance in Scene 8, which in its ultimate
form begins simply with her recitative complaints about life as a
servant. (A cavatina here would have upstaged Despina's
mistresses, neither of whom has had an aria yet.) The original
libretto reveals second thoughts even in the extant aria for
Despina, which was not set as Da Ponte had envisaged. The first
three lines of text:

> In Uomini, in Soldati,
> Sperare fedeltà?
> Non vi fate sentir per carità!
>
> (*Così fan tutte*, No. 12: To expect fidelity, in men, in soldiers?
> For pity's sake, don't let anyone hear you!)

were clearly supposed to have concluded the preceding recitative:
they remain in the *versi sciolti* typical of recitative, and indentation
in the libretto starts only with the lines 'Di pasta simile / Son tutti
quanti. . .' Mozart made an orchestrally accompanied transition out

of what should have been the recitative cadence, allowing Despina to repeat her lines with exaggerated incredulity.

Within Act II, paper-type is of little help in determining the order of composition, though gaps in this part of the autograph – the serenade, No. 21; the accompanied recitative preceding Fiordiligi's *rondò*, No. 25; and No. 30 – possibly indicate that these portions of the music were written quite late. It is certainly surprising that the 'Andante' in which Alfonso proclaims the motto of the opera's title might have been a last-minute addition, yet this is supported by the title page of an early copyist's score, which originally bore no title other than *La Scuola degli Amanti*. Though Da Ponte had further reason to suppress the work's main title (see above), it is tempting to think, along with Tyson, 'that the title *Così fan tutte* was Mozart's inspiration. . .perhaps being adopted only after No. 30. . .had been set to music.'

Space does not permit a discussion here of the extant sketches for the second finale, but some loose ends in the score demand our attention, in so far as they reveal Mozart changing his mind about important musical and dramatic issues. The accompanied recitative preceding No. 26, during which Guglielmo apprises Ferrando of the faithlessness of his beloved Dorabella, had originally ended with Ferrando's plea 'dammi consiglio' (give me advice), and a firm cadence in C minor. But Mozart subsequently extended the recitative to a cadence on D, elided to the four bars of dominant harmony at the start of Guglielmo's G-major aria 'Donne mie, la fate a tanti'. Tyson asks whether Ferrando's aria 'Tradito, schernito' (No. 27) might originally have come here; that piece begins in C minor, and would have followed logically upon Ferrando's elaborately prepared cadence. 'But when Ferrando has asked for advice, it may have struck Mozart that it would be undramatic for him to prevent such advice being given by singing a cavatina; it would be more effective for Guilelmo to tender his counsel at this point in an aria on the subject of woman's nature.'[31] According to this theory, 'Tradito, schernito' was delayed until the next scene and provided with a new accompanied recitative. A similar tonal disjunction, between Dorabella's aria 'È Amore un ladroncello', No. 28 (in B♭) and the end of the preceding recitative (a tritone away, in E) was corrected only in copyists' scores, not in Mozart's autograph – though the new version may derive from him. If the aria we know replaced an earlier one in a different key, as Tyson surmises, then this would seem to have been done only after the composition of No. 30, for

Dorabella's final line, 'Che anch'io farò così', is a first-person conjugation of the motto of the opera.

More noticeable to the listener than these rough spots, which were smoothed over before the opera reached the stage, is a pseudo-quotation in the second finale that refers back to music the listener has never heard. The passage comes shortly after the officers' unexpected return, as they reveal to their fiancées, through ironic quotation of music each had sung while in disguise, that they are the very same 'strangers' with whom the women have just signed marriage contracts. Two of the three passages are recognizable excerpts from earlier numbers, but the first one, during which Ferrando makes 'affected compliments' and introduces himself as the 'Cavaliere dell'Albania', bears no relation to any preceding music or text. As Daniel Heartz has argued, on both musical and dramatic grounds,[32] the most logical origin for Ferrando's D-minor introduction is No. 13 in Act I, in which the two suitors had presented themselves with comic formality to Despina, but not even informally to the two sisters. If the five bars for Ferrando in the finale came from a sacrificed portion of this long, multipartite ensemble, then Mozart must have had too little time to replace them with music from elsewhere in that character's role, or little inclination to alter what is otherwise a delightful and effective moment in the finale.

Towards the première

As *Così* was being readied for performance, a sample libretto was printed, on paper of inferior quality, probably for proofreading purposes and for submission to the censor. The presence of Guglielmo's 'Rivolgete a lui lo sguardo' points to a date before the end of December 1789, though the title page gives the date 1790, in anticipation of the première. In the definitive libretto, produced after Mozart had replaced Guglielmo's first-act aria, the first line of the original version is included by mistake at the end of the preceding recitative, as are also two quatrains of the replacement that were not set by Mozart. The recitative before Fiordiligi's *rondò*, and the beginning of the second finale likewise contained lines left unset by the composer. There are also two apparent interventions by the censor, both in lines sung by Despina. In I/10, both the first libretto and Mozart's score show her rebuffing Alfonso's offer to do her good with the lines 'A una fanciulla / Un vecchio come lei non può far nulla' (an old man like you cannot do anything to a girl); as revised, this became simply 'Un uomo come lei. . .' (a man like you. . .). Similarly, in her aria 'Una donna a quindici anni' (No. 19) at the start of the second act, her statement that a young woman should know, among other things, 'Dove il diavolo ha la coda' (where the Devil keeps his tail) was replaced in the second printing by the harmless but useless phrase 'Quel che il cor più brama e loda' (that which the heart most desires and praises). In both cases, it is impossible to say whether the censor's injunctions were actually followed in performance.

Towards the end of December we find Mozart cancelling a musical evening with Puchberg (as guest) and the violinist Joseph Zistler, saying, 'I have too much work.'[33] Mozart's haste as the première approached is confirmed in a little-known account by his composition pupil Joseph Eybler, remembered today mainly as the person to whom Constanze Mozart first gave her late husband's Requiem for completion. In an autobiographical sketch published in 1826, Eybler explained that Mozart was the unwitting cause of his forswearing a career in the theatre:

For when Mozart wrote the opera *Così fan tutte*, and was not yet finished with the instrumentation, and time was short besides, he requested that I rehearse the singers, and in particular the two female vocalists Fer[r]arese and Villeneuve; whereby I had opportunity enough to become acquainted with theatre life, with its disorders, cabals and so forth. . .[34]

The faint-hearted Eybler was probably assisted in the theatre by the librettist, and by deputy Kapellmeister Joseph Weigl, who had helped rehearse both *Figaro* and *Don Giovanni*.[35]

One aspect of the musical preparations can be followed quite directly in the copyist's score used by Mozart in rehearsals and performances: namely, autograph cuts in the musical text. These included two long (and repetitive) passages in the first finale (bars 461–75, 515–85), and Ferrando's entire aria 'Ah lo veggio', No. 24. (It was also probably in rehearsal, as he saw that Despina required more time to accomplish her Mesmerian cure, that Mozart added the woodwind repeat of the accompaniment to her previous phrase.) Most surprising of all is Mozart's replacement of the canonic toast ('E nel tuo, nel mio bicchiero') in the second-act finale with a noncanonic setting of the same text, based on musical material in the section just preceding (bars 158 ff.). The substitution is preserved in Mozart's hand, on a sheet that was apparently inserted in the performance score.

Despite the supposed cabals of Salieri, time pressures and the difficult personalities and vocal limitations of at least some of the singers, *Così fan tutte* went into performance on 26 January 1790 and was well received. The circumstances which limited the number of performances – the emperor's death, followed shortly by the end of the opera season – have to this day coloured the public's perception of this opera's success. And it is sad to report also that Mozart seems not to have received the fee he expected for the opera. In his 'begging letter' to Puchberg (quoted in Chapter 1) Mozart had stated that, 'according to the current arrangement', during January he would receive 200 ducats – 900 florins or gulden, at that date. Dexter Edge has recently located weekly ledgers from the Viennese theatres for the 1789/90 season in which payment of Mozart's fee for *Così* is recorded, and the amount is 450 florins, not 900.[36] Edge points to cases in which Salieri and Cimarosa were given double or even triple the customary 100 ducats for their operas, and speculates that Mozart may have been promised a similar fee for *Così* (or thought that he had been), and that this may not have been honoured after Joseph's death. It is likewise possible that Mozart's claim about a 200-ducat fee represented wishful thinking; in any case, the amount paid him was a mere 50 florins more than the sum he was asking to borrow from Puchberg.

3 *Synopsis*

The many literary quotations, allusions and proverbs in Da Ponte's Italian text to *Così fan tutte* make it less readily translatable than many other opera buffa librettos. It is perhaps for this reason that the libretto was available in 'Italian only' (bloß italiänisch), as one reads on the poster for the first performance (see Plate 1). It follows that any English-language synopsis will inevitably convey the humour and richness of the original text only imperfectly.

Though Guglielmo's aria 'Rivolgete a lui lo sguardo' was replaced well before the première, in modern performances of *Così* it has sometimes been reinstated, and is thus included here. On this and other changes of plan during the work's composition, and on cuts during the original production, see Chapters 2 and 7, respectively.

Scenic directions below follow the Neue Mozart-Ausgabe (NMA), which conflates the indications in the original libretto and the autograph score. The numbering of pieces, however, follows the more traditional scheme of the 1941 C. F. Peters edition by Georg Schünemann and Kurt Soldan (reprinted 1983 by Dover, New York).

Cast of characters

FIORDILIGI	woman from Ferrara living in Naples, in love with Guglielmo	Adriana Ferrarese del Bene, soprano
DORABELLA	woman from Ferrara living in Naples, in love with Ferrando	Louise Villeneuve, soprano
GUGLIELMO	officer, in love with Fiordiligi	Francesco Benucci, bass
FERRANDO	officer, in love with Dorabella	Vincenzo Calvesi, tenor
DESPINA	the women's maidservant	Dorothea Bussani, soprano
DON ALFONSO	old philosopher	Francesco Bussani, bass

Chorus of soldiers

Chorus of servants

Chorus of sailors

The scene is Naples and its environs.

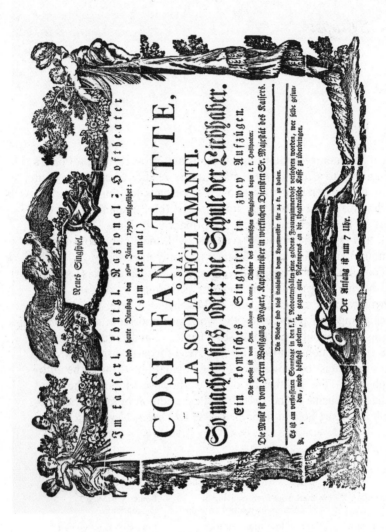

1 Poster for the 1790 première of *Cosi fan tutte* in the Burgtheater, Vienna.

Act I

Stage setting: a coffeehouse.

Overture (C major, Andante ¢ –Presto ¢)

The overture to *Così fan tutte*, like that to *Don Giovanni*, includes music heard near the end of the action. In the opening Andante the plot is foreshadowed through an alternation of ardent lyricism in the solo oboe, accompanied by winds, and punctuating *forte* 'objections' from the full orchestra (representing the women?); from the rhythm of the ensuing cadence, astute spectators would have known mentally to underlay the words of the opera's title. Early in the brilliant Presto that follows, the auditors are meant to fill in a longer version of the same motto: 'Così fan tutte le belle', sung by Basilio to essentially the same motif in No. 7 of *Le nozze di Figaro*. The fast section of the overture is a nearly monothematic sonata movement, characterized by the tossing of short, 'flighty' motifs between the wind instruments, singly and in pairs: 'constancy in inconstancy alone', as Ulybyshev described it.[1] Near the end the motto returns in doubled note values, showing that the tempo relation between Andante and Presto is two-to-one.

Scene 1

Again as in *Don Giovanni*, the opening numbers in *Così* are linked so as to form a modified *introduzione* (a multipartite action ensemble at the beginning of a comic opera); the second and third trios lack opening ritornellos, and the keys of all three outline the opera's tonic triad, G–E–C.

No. 1 Terzetto (Ferrando, Guglielmo, Alfonso: *La mia Dorabella / Capace non è*; G major, Allegro C)

Da Ponte begins the exposition *in medias res*, sketching in information on identities and relationships with a few deft strokes. The philosopher Alfonso, speaking *'ex cathedra'*, has cast doubt on the fidelity of Ferrando's Dorabella and Guglielmo's Fiordiligi; the officers draw their swords (another echo of *Don Giovanni*) and demand proofs. Alfonso comments in an aside on their foolish desire to go looking for what will only make them miserable.

Recitativo

Don Alfonso, who claims to duel only with knife and fork, asks if their fiancées are goddesses, or flesh and blood – an opposition recurrent throughout the opera.

No. 2 Terzetto (Alfonso, Ferrando, Guglielmo: *È la fede delle femmine*; E major, Allegro ¢)

The dictum 'jokingly' adduced here – 'The faith of lovers is like the Arabian phoenix' – is proverbial, but Alfonso has it by way of Metastasio: an entire quatrain taken his opera *Demetrio* of 1731; 'everyone says it exists, but no one knows where to find it'. Each officer insists that his fiancée is the phoenix.

Recitativo

Ferrando and Guglielmo recognize the quotation, dismissing it as 'poetic nonsense' and 'old men's foolishness'. They respond with alacrity to their friend's challenge to give reasons for their faith in their women: 'long experience', 'noble education', 'lofty thoughts', 'analogous temperaments', and so forth, to which Alfonso sarcastically adds 'tears, sighs, caresses', and 'swooning'. Alfonso wagers a hundred sequins that he can show that these women are just like all the others. Guglielmo asks Ferrando what he would do with his share of the winnings.

No. 3 Terzetto (Ferrando, Guglielmo, Alfonso: *Una bella serenata*; C major, Allegro C)

'I will give my goddess a beautiful serenade', Ferrando answers, after a moment's hesitation, during which the orchestra waits on the dominant. The more mundane Guglielmo will honour his Venus with a banquet, to which Alfonso, too, will be invited. Their promise to toast the god of love is accompanied by a frothy full-orchestral trill, a variant of the *Così*-trill of the overture. An ample closing ritornello (a late addition to the score) rounds off the *introduzione* as a whole, providing needed exit music for the men.

Scene 2

Stage setting: a garden on the seashore.

No. 4 Duetto (Fiordiligi, Dorabella: *Ah guarda, sorella*; A major, Andante 3/8–Allegro 2/4)

The two sisters admire locket portraits of their respective lovers, differentiating their descriptions slightly but significantly within what is otherwise a pointedly symmetrical duet. With unwitting foresight, they ask Cupid to condemn them to a living torture should they ever change affections. Fiordiligi quickly declaims these final lines of text while Dorabella sustains a high note on 'penar' (suffer) for nine bars, then they switch parts. This implicit demonstration of their interchangeability has a pendant in the duettino No. 7, for the men.

Recitativo

Fiordiligi is in a 'crazy' mood this morning; here Da Ponte evokes the 'folle journée' of *Figaro*. Taking Dorabella's hand, Fiordiligi reads her fortune: an 'M' and a 'P', for 'matrimony pending'. Expecting their tardy lovers, instead they see Don Alfonso approach, gloomy of countenance.

Scene 3

No. 5 Aria (Alfonso: *Vorrei dir, e cor non ho*; F minor, Allegro agitato ¢)

Alfonso's entrance, weeping, alarms the women; he prolongs their torment in a miniature aria specifically about his inability to utter the terrible news he has for them.

Recitativo

Still sadistically slow to allay the women's fears, Alfonso uses the inverted word order common in Italian poetry to say 'Dead. . .they are not'; nor are they wounded, but rather, called to the battlefield. (No enemy is specified.) Supposedly lacking the courage to face their beloveds, Guglielmo and Ferrando are nevertheless waiting in the wings for Alfonso's signal to enter.

Scene 4

The sequence of five pieces (one of them repeated) associated with the men's departure, in this and the next two scenes, was meant to exploit the comic situation to the utmost. But Mozart heightens the emotional charge, emphasizing the scene's wistful aspects, and the voluptuousness of the seaside setting. The emotional tone is all the more ambiguous in that both text and music are sprinkled with references to embarkation scenes in Mozart's own *Idomeneo*.

No. 6 Quintetto (Guglielmo, Ferrando, Alfonso, Fiordiligi,
Dorabella: *Sento, o Dio, che questo piede*; E♭ major, Andante ¢)

The soldiers feign timidity, but their distraught fiancées urge them to be courageous, and (steering the music to the black key of B♭ minor) implore them to plunge their daggers into their hearts. Ferrando and Guglielmo take this as proof of their constancy, but Alfonso counsels patience: 'finem lauda' (he who laughs last. . .). All then lament how destiny frustrates the hopes of mortals.

Recitativo

Fiordiligi asks Guglielmo to leave his sword behind, so she may use it on herself should he perish; Dorabella says she would need no weapon, as she would die of grief. (Spectators might easily put a more carnal interpretation on all this talk of daggers and swords, reminiscent of Ariosto's *Orlando furioso*.) The men croon comforting phrases to their lovers, in completely parallel writing which announces the texture of the following number.

No. 7 Duettino (Ferrando, Guglielmo: *Al fato dan legge*; B♭
major, Andante 2/4)

The conventionality of the text here ('Those fair eyes impose their will on fate; Love protects them, the barbarous stars dare not disturb their repose. . .') is matched by that of the music; the audience is in no doubt that the men are play-acting. Yet at a near-quotation from the 'great quartet' of *Idomeneo* ('Il ciglio sereno. . .') Mozart permits himself some sincere-sounding chromaticism, underscored by the winds. Humour returns as cadential perorations – beginning with traded melismas on the word 'tornar' (return) – repeatedly frustrate the melody's return to the tonic.

Recitativo

In an aside, Don Alfonso expresses satisfaction at the soldiers' performances. A drum announces the imminent departure of the troop ship, at which news Fiordiligi and Dorabella swoon (so they claim), using stereotypical words and tones nearly identical to those employed by Donna Anna in *Don Giovanni* as she discovers her father's corpse.

Scene 5

No. 8 Coro ('di soldati e cittadini') (*Bella vita militar!*; D major, Maestoso ¢)

The gradual arrival of the troops is composed into the dynamic markings of this march. Its description of military life is ironic (though less so than that in its model, Figaro's 'Non più andrai, farfallone amoroso'), and conducive to word-painting ('fifes', 'bombs').

Recitativo

A further exchange of stereotypical endearments causes the men to miss the main boat to their ship, and they prepare to depart on a smaller vessel.

No. 9 Recitativo (Fiordiligi, Dorabella, Guglielmo, Ferrando, Alfonso: *Di. . .scri. . .ver. . .mi. . .ogni. . .gior. . .no*; F major, Andante C)

This text, composed by Da Ponte out of recitative verses (though with generous use of rhyme), Mozart set as a concerted number, pushing the humour somewhat into the background. In broken phrases (indicated also in the typography of the libretto) Fiordiligi asks Guglielmo to write her every day; twice daily, Dorabella pleads to Ferrando; it is all Alfonso can do to keep from bursting out laughing. But from Fiordiligi's phrase 'Be true to me alone', the music embarks on a rapturous development, whose culmination anticipates a chromatic cadential phrase in Mozart's 'Ave verum corpus' of 1791.

No. 8 Coro [da capo] (*Bella vita militar!*; D major, Maestoso ¢)

During a reprise of the march, the women watch, immobile, as the barque departs with their fiancés.

Scene 6

Recitativo

The men wave farewell, as Don Alfonso and the women express their hope for a safe voyage and speedy return.

No. 10 Terzettino (Fiordiligi, Dorabella, Alfonso: *Soave sia il vento*; E major, [Andante] ¢)

These thoughts are given more lyric expansion in a number whose key and general affect recall two breeze-related numbers from *Idomeneo* (the chorus 'Placido è il mar, andiamo', and Ilia's aria 'Zeffiretti lusinghieri'). The ladies exit.

Scene 7

Recitativo

Left alone, Alfonso congratulates himself on his acting skills. Perhaps prompted by the previous number's talk of sea travel (and now accompanied by the orchestra), he quotes the Renaissance poet Sannazaro, who had said that placing one's faith in women is as futile as ploughing the waves, sowing the sands, and catching the wind in nets.

Scene 8

Stage setting: elegant room with various seats, a small table, etc. Three doors: two at the sides, one in the centre.

Recitativo

It is the next morning. Despina enters lamenting her servant's lot, like Leporello at the start of *Don Giovanni*. She sneaks a taste of her patronesses' chocolate, which normally she may only smell.

Scene 9

The two sisters enter in a state of distraction, and tearing from themselves all feminine ornaments. Fiordiligi demands a dagger, or some poison.

No. 11 Recitative and Aria (Dorabella: *Ah scostati, paventa il tristo effetto. . .Smanie implacabili, che m'agitate*; E♭ major, Allegro agitato ₵)

Continuing in this vein, Dorabella brushes aside Despina, and gives vent to her despair. If she remains alive, the 'horrible sound' of her sighs (illustrated in both the declamation and the accompaniment) will serve as an example to the Eumenides (furies).

Recitativo

The sisters are shocked by their maid's suggestion that they 'divert' themselves with other men during their fiancés' absence. 'One man is as good as another', Despina says, 'because all men are worthless'; at the battlefront, Guglielmo and Ferrando are hardly likely to be faithful.

No. 12 Aria (Despina: *In uomini, in soldati*; F major, Allegretto 2/4, 6/8)

In lines originally meant as recitative, Despina scoffs at her mistresses' idea that men – soldiers, even! – would be faithful. In the aria proper (in 6/8), she enumerates the ways in which they are deceitful, and says that women should 'pay back in similar coin': by loving only at their convenience, or for vanity's sake.

Scene 10

Recitativo

Alfonso ponders how to put his plan into effect. Fearing that Despina may recognize the soldiers in the disguises he has had them don, Alfonso decides to solicit her aid – but not to reveal the identities of the maskers, as is later made clear. With the aid of a bribe and some cajoling, he persuades her to introduce his friends to the ladies.

Scene 11

No. 13 Sestetto

To mark the beginning of the masquerade, Da Ponte and Mozart created a large, multisectional ensemble using finale techniques (though only a single poetic metre).

13.1 (Alfonso: *Alla bella Despinetta*; C major–V/F major,
Allegro C)

To music of a certain formality (a march-like parody of Don
Giovanni's phrase 'Andiam, andiam, mio bene'), Alfonso presents
his friends to the maid, yet without naming them. They kiss her
hand and offer extravagant compliments, and request her aid in
wooing their beloveds. Despina is taken aback by their strange
manners, clothes and moustaches; they seem to be either Turks or
Wallachians (topical references, for Viennese of 1790). The men
express relief that she apparently has not seen through the disguises.
As Fiordiligi and Dorabella are heard approaching, Alfonso with-
draws in order to observe from the wings.

13.2 (Fiordiligi, Dorabella: *Ragazzaccia tracotante*; F
major–V/C minor, Allegro 3/4)

The ladies upbraid their maid for allowing men into their chambers,
and order that they leave. Despina, mindful of her promised
reward, joins the suitors in pleading for indulgence, as the music
turns to A minor. The women react with astonishment – though
more to the beauty of the music, at first, than to the audacity of the
strangers' suit.

13.3 (Fiordiligi, Dorabella: *Ah che più non ho ritegno*; C major,
Molto Allegro ¢)

The sisters' fury explodes with full force, in rapid scales up and
down. Ferrando and Guglielmo delight in this evidence of their
women's faithfulness, but Despina and Alfonso remain sceptical;
significantly, the latter voices his suspicions (bars 141 ff.) to the
same motif he had used in No. 2 to cast doubt on the fidelity of
women ('Che vi sia, ciascun lo dice. . .').

Recitativo

Ostensibly attracted by the noise of the women's protests (and of
Mozart's closing ritornello), Alfonso enters and asks what the trouble
is. 'Men in our house!' Dorabella exclaims, to which the philosopher
answers 'What's the harm?' Only then does he notice his 'dear
friends'; they are slow to respond to his enquiries concerning their

arrival ('You here? how? why? when? in what manner?'), so he prompts them in an aside: 'Play along with me.' The suitors renew their pleas, now in antique-sounding accompanied recitative, and even more extravagant language.

No. 14 Recitative and Aria (Fiordiligi: *Temerari, sortite. . .Come scoglio immoto resta*; B♭ major, Andante maestoso C–Allegro–Più Allegro C)

Fiordiligi takes the lead in repulsing the intruders, warning them not to profane their hearts, their ears, their affections; she and her sister will be faithful to their fiancés unto death. But Mozart undermines her utterances by expanding her vocal leaps to the point of parody – of Ferrarese herself (who was known for her wide range), and of a recent opera by Salieri in which she had displayed this gift (see Chapter 7).

The aria, too, teeters on the edge between seriousness and farce. Its text harks back to metaphor arias of opera seria, but here the first two clauses ('As a rock stands firm agains the winds and the storm, so this soul is firm in its faith and in its love') are set in a fairly ridiculous musical syntax, straddling a sectional division (see Chapter 6). In a final stretta section Mozart suggests Fiordiligi's state of near-hysteria, with initial five-bar phrases, long melismas in triplets, and a sudden outburst on high B♭. Fiordiligi, accompanied by her sister, starts to leave the stage – as singers normally did after a bravura aria, but the women are detained by Ferrando and Guglielmo.

Recitativo

Don Alfonso asks the women not to make him look foolish; all the strangers desire is a bit of kindness. Guglielmo quickly adds that they will die at the women's feet if refused this favour.

No. 15a Aria (Guglielmo: *Rivolgete a lui lo sguardo*; D major–V^7/G, Allegro C–Allegro molto C)

No. 15 Aria (Guglielmo: *Non siate ritrosi*; G major–V^7/G, Andantino 2/4)

Da Ponte's and Mozart's first instinct here was to write a show-stopper for Benucci, on the order of his aria 'Non più andrai, farfallone amoroso' in *Le nozze di Figaro*. In this aria, as in the one that replaced it, Guglielmo vaunts those of his and Ferrando's features that appeal to ladies. The differences between the two are of length, scoring (full orchestra with trumpets, in the first case), language, and in one important respect, plot: in the rejected aria, Guglielmo already crosses the original pairs of lovers, directing Fiordiligi's gaze to Ferrando, and Dorabella's to himself. His comparisons of Ferrando and himself to figures both mythical and modern (they are as fair as Narcissus, as rich as Croesus, as strong as Cyclops, and as nimble as the ballet dancer Le Picq) were as many invitations for musical illustration by Mozart. Guglielmo's final risqué boast of one further asset sends the ladies running off in anger (this too being painted in the music), much to his delight.

The replacement aria is considerably shorter than 'Rivolgete a lui lo sguardo', and devoid of the earlier number's topical references. Equally important, it did not anticipate the tonality of the finale to come, as had the rejected piece. Altogether lighter in style and scoring, 'Non siate ritrosi' emphasizes the men's physical attractions in language more comic than suggestive. Only Guglielmo's final comment, that their moustaches might be considered plumes of love, is sufficient to send the women scurrying.

2 Francesco Benucci, the first Guglielmo (engraving by F. John after a painting by Dorffmeister)

Scene 12

No. 16 Terzetto (Alfonso, Ferrando, Guglielmo: *E voi ridete?*;
G major, Molto Allegro 3/4)

This laughing-trio issues directly from whichever of the two arias is
sung by Guglielmo. In No. 9 it was Alfonso who could barely
restrain his mirth; now he seeks to prevent his friends from laughing
so loudly that they spoil the charade. In any case, he knows their
laughter will only end in tears.

Recitativo

The confident lovers desire no further proof, and wish to receive
their winnings, or even a portion of them. Alfonso mocks their naïveté, and requires their obedience until the next morning. Guglielmo
wonders if this means they will not eat that day; for Ferrando, the
supper will be all the more appetizing once the battle is won.

No. 17 Aria (Ferrando: *Un'aura amorosa*; A major, Andante
cantabile 3/8)

Ferrando develops this thought further, saying that a mere breath of
love from his fair one will suffice; his heart requires no other
nourishment. The aria is another of this opera's *surprises de l'amour*
(to use Marivaux's expression): pieces such as 'Di scrivermi ogni
giorno' whose ravishing musical beauties, in the service of love, catch
both spectator and singer unawares. Prepared by a mere two lines of
recitative, and a single flourish from the strings, 'Un'aura amorosa'
reveals a hitherto unsuspected depth of feeling in Ferrando. As with
the serenade, No. 21, the music here is signally successful in making
one forget how thoroughly conventional the poetry is. The aria con-
cludes with exalted exit music of a sort that Mozart used sparingly.

Scene 13

Recitativo

Despina reports to Alfonso that her mistresses are in the garden,
complaining to the breezes and the flies that their lovers have
departed. Were she in their place, instead of crying she would laugh,
and replace the one absent lover with two others. The philosopher
encourages her cynicism (which suits his purposes), and she continues

with a frankly hedonist definition of love. As Alfonso is at a loss as to how to proceed, Despina now takes over the direction of the intrigue; she has already led a thousand men by the nose, and doing so with two women will pose no problem.

This scene was often cut in early productions of the opera. But it is important for the drama, in that Despina's attitudes are subtly distinguished from those of Alfonso, who has a larger goal in view than just leading a successful seduction; the differences are thrown in relief at the dénouement.

Scene 14

Stage setting: elegant garden. Two turf benches at the sides.

No. 18 Finale
18.1 (Fiordiligi, Dorabella: *Ah che tutta in un momento*;
D major, [Andante] 2/4)

The two sisters make a show of sulking, though the coquettish woodwind figures and frequent sighs of the long opening ritornello reveal other feelings as well. When they sing to this same music, however, it is with the most stereotypical of lamentations from opera seria ('Ah, what a sea of torments my life has become. . .') – an intentionally amusing incongruity. The continuation of their melody is given a conspicuous horn accompaniment, the implications of which are by now clear.

Scene 15

18.2 (Ferrando, Guglielmo: *Si mora sì, si mora*; G minor,
Allegro ¢)

Ferrando and Guglielmo are heard offstage threatening suicide, as Alfonso tries to dissuade them. They enter and make a show of swallowing arsenic, in order (they say) to be free of the ladies' cruelty. The suitors then urge the sisters to draw near and observe what their indifference has brought about.

18.3 (Alfonso: *Giacchè a morir vicini*; E♭ major, [Allegro ¢])

Alfonso advises the ladies to show some pity, but instead they cry for help. Despina hears their call, and she advises no differently:

they must hold the unfortunates in their arms while she and Alfonso seek a doctor. In simultaneous asides the as yet unwilling sisters comment on the terrible position this puts them in, while the suitors delight in the comic spectacle of it all.

18.4 (Ferrando, Guglielmo: *Ah!* / Fiordiligi, Dorabella: *Sospiran gli infelici*; C minor, [Allegro ¢])

Musically the development section of the finale, this section is also the opera's turning point. Rapid modulations over a repeated heartbeat-motif reflect the weakening resolve of the two women, left alone with the prone and sighing strangers. Cautiously they approach these 'figure interessanti' ('interesting' in the eighteenth-century sense: touching, affecting). Each feels the cold forehead of the other's fiancé, and checks his pulse. *Sotto voce*, the men note how both women have become more amenable, as the latter admit (to the accompaniment of lascivious rising chromatics) that the men's deaths would cause them to weep.

Scene 16

18.5 (Alfonso: *Eccovi il medico, / Signore belle*; G major, Allegro 3/4)

Help arrives in the form of Despina, masquerading as a doctor. The soldiers see through her disguise immediately; they may have been tipped off, but it is the music that betrays the chambermaid to the audience, with the same motif that had introduced her first aria. Despina greets the ladies in bad Latin, and boasts comically of knowing many other languages besides (including Swabian, the dialect spoken by Anton Mesmer). She ascertains the nature, dosage and temperature of the poison, and reassures Alfonso and the ladies that the patients are in good hands. She cures them not with an antidote, but with a Mesmeric magnet. As this causes the men violent tremors, she instructs the women to hold firm their brows.

18.6 (Ferrando, Guglielmo: *Dove son, che loco è questo!*; B♭ major, Andante C)

A third-relation at the start of this section shows the strangers' disorientation as they awaken. Are these fair creatures Athena and

Venus? The men soon recognise their beloveds (NB: in the new pairing), and begin kissing their hands. (The leaders of the charade excuse their behaviour as a residual effect of the poison.) The women protest mildly, but privately admit to being sorely tempted, as the men again must restrain themselves from laughing.

18.7 (Ferrando, Guglielmo: *Dammi un bacio o mio tesoro*; D major, Allegro / Presto ¢)

The men now demand a kiss, or they will die on the spot. This Fiordiligi and Dorabella find too outrageous, and their anger prompts amused asides from the four characters in the know. However Ferrando and Guglielmo rightly wonder if this anger is feigned or real. It is the business of the next act to resolve their doubt, one way or the other; for the moment, the situation provides the expected noisy conclusion to one of Da Ponte and Mozart's most varied and comical finales.

Act II

Scene 1

Stage setting: a room [that of Act I, Scene 8 ff.].

Recitativo

Despina, now undisguised, tries to convince her mistresses to act like the women they are: by treating love as a trifle, by choosing when to be constant and when not to. Until their fiancés return from the war, they should 'go recruiting'; women such as they can do without love, but not without lovers. Fiordiligi and Dorabella are outraged, but hear her out. Quite aside from the immorality of what their maid proposes, Fiordiligi is troubled by more pragmatic considerations: people will talk, and their fiancés will find out. Despina answers that she will simply spread it about that the men are calling on her; though sceptical, the sisters wish to hear more.

No. 19 Aria (Despina: *Una donna a quindici anni*; G major, Andante 6/8–Allegretto 6/8)

It is as much on account of this lesson in feminine wiles, as Alfonso's later admonishments to the men in No. 30, that Da Ponte gave his opera the subtitle 'The school for lovers'. Like her first aria, this one is in 6/8 metre (often an indicator of low social status), and is a catalogue, this time of the essential tricks that will make men fall in love. These include: knowing how to feign laughter and tears, to invent excuses, to lie without blushing, and to give hope to all comers, be they handsome or ugly. Despina's aria recalls Osmin's 'Solche hergelauf'ne Laffen' in *Die Entführung aus dem Serail*, both in its use of mock-seria style (as she speaks of commanding obedience, like a queen), and in its teasing coda, after the piece is seemingly over. Despina leaves the stage remarking that the sisters appear to like her 'doctrine'.

Scene 2

Recitativo

Left alone, the women restate their objections, as if to convince themselves of their validity. Dorabella is the first to go over to Despina's viewpoint, reassuring her sister that their hearts will remain as they are; 'by amusing ourselves a bit, and not dying of melancholy, we're not being unfaithful'. As they choose which stranger each will favour, the more cautious Fiordiligi tells her sister to go first; Dorabella admits that she has already decided.

No. 20 Duetto (Dorabella: *Prenderò quel brunettino*; B♭ major, Andante 2/4)

In much the same way that they had compared portraits of their original lovers in No. 4, the sisters now describe their new gallants, in terms that show their intention to make light of the whole affair. In mocking fashion they predict the sighs and endearments they expect to hear – quite accurately, as it turns out.

Scene 3

Recitativo

Alfonso enters and tells the ladies to hurry to the garden, where the strangers have prepared an enchanting serenade.

Scene 4

Stage setting: garden on the seashore with turf benches and two small stone tables. Barque adorned with flowers, with group of instrumentalists.

No. 21 Duetto con coro (Ferrando, Guglielmo: *Secondate aurette amiche*; E♭ major, Andante 3/8)

Returning to a device used with success in *Don Giovanni*, Da Ponte and Mozart deploy a wind band on stage (in a flower-bedecked boat). Pairs of horns, bassoons, and clarinets are joined not by the usual oboes, but – this being another 'breeze' piece – by flutes, which are reserved for the coda with chorus. In fact there is a steady crescendo of musical forces (winds alone, joined first by the suitors, and then by the chorus), in an attempt to overwhelm the ladies' senses. The words the men sing might easily have been written by a Zeno or Metastasio: they ask the friendly zephyrs to waft their sighs to their beloveds, and to repeat to them the laments to which they (the winds) have a thousand times borne witness. That this request is made in front of these same women seems odd, intentionally humorous, even; but nothing in the musical setting encourages one to notice this.

Recitativo

Alfonso tells the servants to place their vases of flowers on the tables and to return to their barque, as Fiordiligi and Dorabella wonder what this masquerade can mean. The two strangers claim to be struck dumb by love; their faltering attempts at conversation exasperate Don Alfonso who, with Despina's aid, proceeds to put words in the lovers' mouths.

No. 22 Quartetto (Alfonso: *La mano a me date*; D major, Allegretto grazioso, 6/8–Allegro C–Tempo I 6/8–Presto C)

Properly speaking, this number is not a quartet, but an echo-ensemble such as one often finds in comic opera, and even sacred music (e.g. the 'Audi coelum' of Monteverdi's 1610 Vespers). It is also another of this opera's lessons for lovers, though two of the students only pretend to need instruction. Speaking for the men, Alfonso explains grandiloquently to the ladies that a trembling slave implores [their] forgiveness; he has offended them, but will now limit his desires to that which he can obtain. Ferrando and Guglielmo only manage to repeat the last part of all this. The sisters merely laugh, so Despina answers for them, in accompanied recitative reminiscent of that which preceded Fiordiligi's aria 'Come scoglio': 'What's done is done; let us forget the past, and may that bond [i.e. to their former lovers], symbol of servitude, now be broken.' In an aside (set to a duple-metre variation of the main motif) the puppeteers assert that the women must surely now fall. They leave the lovers on their own.

Scene 5

Recitativo

After an embarrassed silence, the two couples revert to inane small-talk. Fiordiligi suggests a stroll to Ferrando, and Dorabella follows suit with Guglielmo. Guglielmo pretends to feel unwell; Dorabella steels herself against the coming assault, and says that his illness must be a lingering affect of the poison. She makes light of his rejoinder: that what he has drunk from her 'fiery Mount Etnas of love' (her eyes) is a far stronger poison. Offended (and noticing with concern the absence of the other pair), Guglielmo demands some sign of her pity. Will she accept his gift of a heart? Apologizing under his breath to Ferrando, he makes another, successful effort to sway her, in a Goldonian burlesque of amorous dialogue.

> No. 23 Duetto (Guglielmo: *Il core vi dono*; F major, Andante grazioso 3/8)

In the first act the sisters are less distinctly characterized than their fiancés. But Da Ponte and Mozart now emphasize the differing levels of resistance they offer when seduced. In the back of spectators' minds, no doubt, during both this duet and No. 29, was 'Là ci darem' from *Don Giovanni*. (Zerlina's heartbeat-aria 'Vedrai, carino' is likewise close at hand.) Dorabella accepts Guglielmo's heart, but cannot reciprocate, as she has given hers away. 'Then why is it beating here', he asks, and within a few measures they are already singing together, their heartbeats in unison. Next he tries to place the heart in her locket, but she says it cannot go there. Understanding that she does not wish to have it in the same place as Ferrando's portrait, Guglielmo turns her head aside and makes the switch. 'I seem to have a Vesuvius in my breast!' she says in an aside that complements his earlier mention of Mount Etna. At this point the music returns to the original motif, with horns now prominently signalling the cuckolding of Ferrando. The new lovers' voices unite in delight at the 'happy exchange'.

Scene 6

In between the two seduction duets, Da Ponte and Mozart place five consecutive arias. This might seem a miscalculation, but more likely it resulted from a deliberate decision to focus on the differing effects of the charade on the four lovers individually, before reverting, for the reconciliation of the original couples, to the ensemble texture which so dominates this opera. It should be noted that the complete lack of simple recitative until after No. 25 contributes greatly to the forward momentum of these solo pieces.

> No. 24 Recitative and Aria (Ferrando: *Barbara, perchè*
> *fuggi?. . .Ah! lo veggio, quell'anima bella*; B♭ major, Allegretto
> ¢–Allegro ¢)

It takes two tries before Ferrando can overcome Fiordiligi's resistance – a reflection of the unshakeable fidelity of the original Fiordiligi in Ariosto's epic poem. Ferrando's first attempt follows immediately upon Dorabella's capitulation; Fiordiligi is in full flight from his advances, as running scales in the orchestra illustrate. She claims to have seen 'an asp, a hydra, a basilisk', but the mythological status of the latter two beasts allows Ferrando easily to guess that she really means him. Fiordiligi's tone softens as she accuses Ferrando of wishing to steal her peace of mind – ironically in a near-quotation of music she had sung to the words 'intact faith' (i.e. to Guglielmo) before her aria 'Come scoglio'. Ferrando persists and, perceiving what he believes to be a sigh, breaks out with an effusive aria.

Ferrando tries to force Fiordiligi to say with her lips what her eyes are already telling him. (The repeated upward thrusts of his melodic line on the word 'rubella' [rebellious] represent her attempts to struggle free.) The rondo form of the piece makes his message all the more insistent, as does also the extraordinarily high tessitura. The aria's technical demands, and the high concentration of arias in this portion of the opera, are perhaps what moved Mozart to cut this number in the first production; many later conductors have done likewise. But this is to be regretted, as without this piece, Fiordiligi's subsequent *rondò* is sorely lacking in motivation.

Scene 7

> No. 25 Recitative and Rondò (Fiordiligi: *Ei parte. . .senti. . .ah*
> *no. . .partir si lasci. . .Per pietà, ben mio, perdona*; E major,
> Adagio C–Allegro moderato C)

Ferrando having left in (feigned) desperation, Fiordiligi is prey to her conflicting sentiments of ardour and remorse. She calls him back, but thinks better of it, and upbraids herself for having given him a hearing. She recognizes that her passion is 'no longer the effect of virtuous love'; but in qualifying it as 'frenzy, anguish, remorse, regret, frivolity, perfidy, and treachery', both she (and the music) cross over into parody. Mozart immediately pulls the listener back in the other direction with an ominous hollow fifth at the cadence.

Fiordiligi's *rondò*, the main showpiece of the opera, begins less obviously tinged with parody than the preceding recitative (or than her earlier 'Come scoglio'). The text is a sustained apology to her original lover. Fiordiligi's melody in the first section again veers between high and low registers, but appropriately, as an expression of her shame. Yet the virtuosic horn solos, beginning at the reprise of this section, hint strongly at infidelity. Beethoven imitated the device in Leonore's principal aria in *Fidelio*, in the same key, using this aria as his model, with no such connotations. By the end of Fiordiligi's *rondò* the reference is all too clear, for the audience, if not for her – particularly at the horns' final outburst, during which Fiordiligi trills on the word 'bene' (beloved).

Scene 8

Recitativo

Alfonso has warned the officers against premature celebrations of victory, but in reporting to Guglielmo on Fiordiligi's steadfastness (as far as he could tell), Ferrando does not imagine that his Dorabella could have behaved any differently. Guglielmo draws out telling him the bad news with as much sadism as Alfonso had used in informing the ladies of their departure in Act I. Ferrando thinks his friend must be joking, until Guglielmo pulls out the portrait Dorabella has given him.

> No. 26 Recitative and Aria (Ferrando: *Il mio ritratto! Ah perfida!*. . .Guglielmo: *Donne mie, la fate a tanti*; G major, Allegretto 2/4)

At this point Ferrando breaks into accompanied recitative, which Mozart gleefully fills with clichés of operatic fury. Ferrando starts to leave, intent on tearing out Dorabella's wicked heart, but Guglielmo restrains him, and asks if it is worth fretting over a woman who 'is not worth two cents'. (These words spoil at the last moment what was set up by Da Ponte as an obscene rhyme.)[2] How can he ever manage to forget her, Ferrando asks. Guglielmo is at a loss for advice.

Though the musical preparation thus far has led one to expect an aria for Ferrando, several further bars of recitative lead instead to a 'philosophical' aria for Guglielmo. 'Women, you do it to so many', and the horn-fifths in the orchestra leave no doubt as to what the 'it' is. Guglielmo wishes women well, and has proved it with both words and deeds, yet cannot forgive them this 'annoying little habit'. On the final return of the refrain, Da Ponte alters the ending so as to echo a couplet concerning Cherubino in his first opera for Mozart (see Chapter 1).

Scene 9

No. 27 Recitative and Cavatina (Ferrando: *In qual fiero contrasto. . .Tradito, schernito*; C minor/E♭ major/C major, Allegro ¢)

Ferrando's scene is a distillation of countless opera arias in which the hero or heroine vacillates between feelings of love and vengeance: Stravinsky found in it the perfect model for Baba the Turk's rage aria in *The rake's progress*. Despite all that Guglielmo has just said, Ferrando perceives his situation as completely 'new and unheard of'. He will have his revenge on Dorabella, he declares, but. . .(again!) how will he ever be able to forget her?

The text of Ferrando's aria – a laconic accusation of betrayal, followed by admission that he still loves his fiancée – closely follows Metastasian archetypes, including their unusual verse-type of strictly accentuated *senari*.[3] Mozart sets the text twice through, placing the two sentiments in different tonal realms (minor for the accusation, relative and then parallel major for the rest), again as in earlier prototypes. Significantly, the 'voices of love' Ferrando still hears are the woodwinds, as in his serenade with Guglielmo, No. 21. As Ferrando reaches the major tonic, Alfonso (absent since Scene 4) and Guglielmo appear at the back of the stage; they stay and listen.

Recitativo

The two spectators enter and tease Ferrando, Guglielmo drawing comparisons favourable to himself. Alfonso will not yet give him his half of the wager, however; first they must make one further attempt.

Ferrando, *im 2.ten Costume aus der Oper: Mädchentreue,*
(Cosi fan tutte) gespielt von Hrn. Grünbaum
        Act.2. Sc.9.
"Verrathen! – verschmacht! – vergessen bin ich!,,

3 Johann Christoff Grünbaum as Ferrando in *Mädchentreue*, a
   German-language version of *Così* by G. F. Treitschke (*Prager
   Theater-Almanach*, 1809)

In antique-style arioso he tells them, in effect, not to count their chickens before they hatch.

Scene 10

Stage setting: room with various doors, mirror, and small table.

Recitativo

Despina congratulates Dorabella (still in a bit of a spin) on having made the most of her amorous opportunity. Fiordiligi enters in a frenzy of guilt, unaware that things have progressed considerably farther with the other couple. Having anticipated that Dorabella and Despina would be horrified at her feelings for the blonde stranger, instead she is horrified at her sister's quick capitulation. Has she forgotten about the poor lovers they have lost just that morning? Dorabella answers, with logic reminiscent of Alfonso's proverb, that there is a considerable difference between a sure thing and the unsure return of their lovers. They are women, Dorabella replies, and there's no use fighting; Fiordiligi should simply give in to love, as she has done.

No. 28 Aria (Dorabella: *È Amore un ladroncello*; B♭ major, Allegretto vivace 6/8)

As was seen in Chapter 2, this aria evidently replaced an earlier piece in a sharp key. But the new number was made integral to the work by virtue of its final section, which ends with a conjugation of the opera's motto: 'If [Love] settles in your heart, do all that he asks, for I shall do so too' (Che anch'io farò così). Having adopted Alfonso's reasoning, Dorabella now takes up Despina's 6/8 metre and philosophy. Her almost anatomical description – reminiscent of much earlier Italian poetry – of how Love gains entry to the soul, is interlarded with several quite licentious *doubles entendres*. Dorabella and Despina exit.

Scene 11

Recitativo

Fiordiligi resolves to ignore her sister's advice and to shun the seducer. Guglielmo, passing by the door at just this moment, overhears and is encouraged by the constancy of his 'Artemisia'. Seized by a sudden inspiration, Fiordiligi calls Despina and orders her to bring the soldiers' extra uniforms, swords, and caps. She will seek out her beloved on the battlefield; perhaps Dorabella will follow her example. Despina leaves to order horses, and to send Dorabella in to talk to her sister.

Scene 12

Recitativo

Da Ponte undercuts any seriousness this moment might have had by making Fiordiligi choose the uniform of her would-be seducer. (Guglielmo either does not notice this, or does not grasp the significance of the choice.) Fiordiligi tears off her feminine headdress, and dons Ferrando's uniform.

> No. 29 Duetto (Fiordiligi: *Fra gli amplessi in pochi istanti*;
> A major, Adagio C–Con più moto–Allegro–Larghetto
> 3/4–Andante ¢)

Ferrando's difficult seduction of Fiordiligi, resumed in this duet, is in marked contrast to Guglielmo's easy conquest of her sister. But at first we are not even aware that this is another seduction duet, for Mozart has led one to expect an aria. Fiordiligi begins after an orchestral flourish (similar to that in Ferrando's first-act aria, and in the same key), singing of her plan to join Guglielmo, and anticipating his joy at seeing her. Just as she reaches the dominant, Ferrando bursts upon the scene, diverting the music to the minor in the process, with complaints that her refusals are condemning him to death. (His words are almost identical to those that the sisters had jokingly predicted in No. 20.) Many more tonal and formal surprises follow. Fiordiligi, stunned into recitative, steers the key to C major, and a nearly literal quotation from Ferrando's 'Una bella serenata' in No. 3 – which she had not heard. He continues the familiar melody, once again asking her to plunge her sword into his breast. A series of short exchanges ensues, after which, singing together, Ferrando notes and Fiordiligi acknowledges her incipient vacillation. The *biondino* pleads even more insistently, as Fiordiligi retreats in confusion to a half-cadence in the minor tonic.

At this point Ferrando tries a different strategy, slowing to a triple-metre Larghetto in the tonic. His lyric quatrain, in which he beseeches Fiordiligi to turn her eyes toward him, is not without humour, however: a lascivious offer to be a 'spouse, lover, and more, if you desire'. Fiordiligi is helpless to resist and, pushed over the edge by a soaring oboe phrase (recalling others in the introduction of the overture, and at the end of Ferrando's No. 17), she tells the stranger to do with her as he wishes. Guglielmo has been a witness to these events, and Alfonso must now restrain him from interfering. Some earlier editions recommend cuts in the lengthy endearments for the lovers in the following, final section, but Mozart's music here is best performed unabridged, in order to balance all the prior instability in this most unorthodox of duets.

Scene 13

Recitativo

Guglielmo vents his rage at the just-departed Fiordiligi ('Fior. . .fior di diavolo'), heaping upon her the worst epithets his brain can imagine. Ferrando cannot resist throwing back at Guglielmo his earlier boasts of possessing 'a little more merit', which supposedly had kept his fiancée true to him while Ferrando's had failed. Alfonso suggests a solution to the soldiers' torment: marry their women. Guglielmo declares he would rather marry Charon's boat, and Ferrando Vulcan's cave. After all, there are plenty of other women in the world. But, Alfonso, asks, how would other women behave, if these ones were unfaithful? The soldiers admit that they still love their fiancées, and meekly submit to Alfonso's lesson on the necessity of 'philosophy' in love.

No. 30 Andante (Alfonso: *Tutti accusan le donne, ed io le scuso*; C major, ¢)

Like many a teacher, Alfonso makes his lesson more memorable by putting it into verse. But rather than choosing an operatic metre, the learned philosopher avails himself of the venerable *ottava rima*, the same form used by Ariosto for his epic *Orlando furioso*. In a loose musical drapery of accompanied recitative bordering on arioso, Alfonso explains that infidelity in women is not to be condemned, as for them it is a 'necessity of the heart'. Men have no cause to feel betrayed, for 'All women are like that' (così fan tutte). Here, at last, the motto of the overture returns, as this maxim is intoned by Alfonso and repeated by his 'students'.

Scene 14

Recitativo

Despina congratulates the bridegrooms-to-be, and informs them that she has told the ladies that the strangers will depart with them in three days' time. They have ordered her to find a notary, and are waiting in their room. The men declare themselves content with the arrangement.

Scene 15

Stage setting: richly illuminated hall, with an orchestra in the background. Table set for four persons with silver candelabra. Four richly attired servants.

No. 31 Finale
31.1 (Despina: *Fate presto o cari amici*; C major, Allegro assai C)

To a bustling orchestral accompaniment, Despina orders the servants to hurry with their preparations; the first violins' trill motif at the beginning recalls that of the first terzetto, helping signal that the action is coming full circle. Alfonso admires the abundance and elegance of the wedding banquet, and on behalf of the bridegrooms promises the servants a large tip.

Scene 16

31.2 (Coro: *Benedetti i doppi coniugi*; E♭ major, Andante ¢)

At the entrance of the bridal couples (in the new pairing), the servants sing benedictions upon them as the orchestra plays a march: 'Like chickens, may they have many children, all equal to them in beauty.' The lovers admire the magnificence spread before them, and give credit to Despina.

31.3 (Ferrando, Guglielmo: *Tutto, tutto o vita mia*; A♭ major, Andante ¢)

The men and women exchange comically trite endearments, and propose a toast.

31.4 (Fiordiligi: *E nel tuo, nel mio bicchiero*; A♭ major,
Larghetto 3/4)

In one of the most glorious moments of Mozart's score, the lovers
drink to oblivion, in music that combines the sensuousness of
Ferrando's 'Volgi a me' in his duet with Fiordiligi with strict canonic
writing. The second half of the text (which is largely submerged in
the counterpoint): 'And let no memory of the past remain', echoes
sentiments Despina had put into the women's mouths in No. 20.
Only Guglielmo refuses to join in, and instead wishes – in an ironic
twist on the first finale – that the two 'vixens' were drinking poison.

Scene 17

31.5 (Alfonso: *Miei signori, tutto è fatto*; E major–A major,
Allegro ¢)

An enharmonic transition and oboe solo usher in Don Alfonso,
with news that the notary is on his way with the contracts. Despina
enters and introduces herself as the notary Beccavivi (literally: 'peck
the living'). Da Ponte gave her all the comic pedantry expected in
an opera buffa lawyer; Mozart, too, clearly delighted in her
assumed character, giving the orchestra eight different accompanimental figurations in succession as she recites the contract to as
many repetitions of the same formula. (Only here do we learn the
Albanians' names: Tizio and Sempronio – Italian equivalents of
'Tom, Dick and Harry', and names still used to denote anonymous
parties in Italian jurisprudence.) Cutting Despina short, the fiancés
declare themselves satisfied, and the ladies (only) sign.

31.6 (Coro: *Bella vita militar!*; D major, Maestoso ¢)

An offstage drumroll and reprise of the military chorus from Act I
interrupt the proceedings, leaving Alfonso holding the contract.
He goes to the window to see what all the noise is about.

31.7 (Alfonso: *Misericordia!*; E♭ major–G minor, Allegro
3/4–[Allegro] ¢)

Feigning horror, Alfonso reports the return of the ladies' original
fiancés. As the servants remove all trace of the wedding banquet,
the women tell the men to flee, but are persuaded to let them hide

instead in an adjacent room, for fear that they will run into their
fiancés. Despina hides in another room. Key, verse-form and motif
all recall the frenzy that followed the poisoning in the first finale.

Scene 18

31.8 (Ferrando, Guglielmo: *Sani e salvi agli amplessi amorosi*;
Bb major–V/Eb, Andante ₵–Con più moto)

The calm good humour shown by the men as they return, wearing
their original uniforms, is in sharp contrast to the women's anxiety.
In answer to Alfonso's string of interrogatives (recalling those with
which he had greeted the 'strangers' after No. 13), the soldiers
explain that they have been recalled by royal command. They ask
why their fiancées are so pale and tongue-tied; speaking for the
ladies, Alfonso says they are overwhelmed with joy at their home-
coming. Guglielmo, depositing his trunk in another room, discovers
Despina the 'notary', who as she unmasks explains that she is returning from a costume ball. Alfonso quietly tells the men to retrieve the
contract he has dropped. Ferrando hands the papers to Guglielmo
to read, which he does with an ostentatious double-take.

31.9 (Ferrando, Guglielmo: *Giusto ciel, voi qui scriveste*; Eb
major, Allegro ₵)

The soldiers erupt in a fit of mock fury, threatening to cause
rivers, seas of blood to flow.

31.10 (Fiordiligi, Dorabella: *Ah signor son rea di morte*; C
minor–V/Bb minor, Andante ₵)

The women admit their guilt and once again beg their fiancés – in
their habitual parallel thirds – to plunge their swords into their
breasts. But in the same breath they blame their failure on the 'cruel'
Alfonso, the 'seductress' Despina. Alfonso says that the proof of
what they say is in the room where the strangers are supposedly hidden; Ferrando and Guglielmo enter, supposedly to see for themselves.

31.11 (Ferrando: *A voi s'inchina*; D minor–V/A minor,
Allegretto ₵)

The men emerge, without their military coats and caps, but wearing
their disguises (minus moustaches). Here begins a series of ironic

recalls of earlier music, in which the unmasked seducers remind the women of key moments in the charade.

But the first of these quotations is of music never actually heard during the opera; Ferrando's grandiloquent self-introduction as an Albanian cavalier can only have come from a number (or part of a number) removed before the opera's completion (see Chapter 2).

31.12 (Guglielmo: *Il ritrattino*; F major–V/F, Andante 3/8)

Next, to the music of No. 23, Guglielmo returns to Dorabella the miniature portrait of Ferrando that she had exchanged for his heart.

31.13 (Ferrando, Guglielmo: *Ed al magnetico*; C major–V/G, Allegretto 3/8)

To the music that had accompanied the doctor's magnetic cure in the first finale (though in halved note values), Ferrando and Guglielmo now give Despina her due. Music that had accompanied the men's convulsions in the earlier finale continues as the sisters express astonishment. Recovering their indignation, they point accusing fingers at Alfonso.

31.14 (Alfonso: *V'ingannai, ma fu l'inganno*; D major–G major, Andante con moto ¢)

The philosopher admits to having deceived the women, but points out that their lovers were undeceived in the process. He reunites the couples, telling them to keep quiet, and laugh, as he is doing. In Edward Dent's account of the opera one reads: 'Whether the ladies pair off with their original lovers or their new ones is not clear from the libretto, but, as Don Alfonso says, it will not make any difference to speak of.'[4] This notion has appealed to several directors, but cannot be taken seriously. For one thing, the women's plea for forgiveness is incomprehensible without a return to the original fiancés. And those who object that Alfonso has just pronounced the couples husbands and wives following the signing of the contract ('Qua le destre: siete sposi') misconstrue the word 'sposo', which means 'betrothed' as well as 'spouse'. In any case, the false marriage contract has no legal force. The sisters promise to make amends through their renewed faith and love; this the men are willing to believe, but – recognizing finally the wisdom of Alfonso's earlier warning – they do not wish to put things to the test. Despina's lines in the ensemble, which are easily overlooked, are significant: confused and ashamed, she admits to having been fooled, and in effect, to having missed seeing Alfonso's larger goal. Just as well, she muses; she has fooled many a person herself.

> 31.15 (Tutti: *Fortunato l'uom che prende*; C major, Allegro
> molto ¢)

All six characters now join to sing the 'philosophical' moral of the opera. Da Ponte and Mozart chose not the misogynist creed represented by the motto 'così fan tutte' (which had been given sufficient exposure), but rather a more generous message of reconciliation. 'Happy is he who looks on the bright side of things, and in all cases lets himself be guided by reason. May that which makes others weep be for him a cause to laugh, and amidst the storms of this world he will find perfect calm.' Thus (in *Orlando furioso*) had Iocondo and Astolfo, after suffering untold torments on account of their wives' infidelities, rationally decided that since 'both are as virtuous as the best, / Let us return and live with them at rest.'

4 The sources of an 'original' libretto

For more than two centuries, Mozartians of various stripes have sought to discover a source for Da Ponte's libretto for *Così fan tutte* – in part because the origins of his texts for *Figaro* and *Don Giovanni* were, by comparison, so clear. Their motivations have varied greatly, but there has generally been an assumption that there was indeed a source to be found, and that its identification would reveal something about Mozart's attitude towards the text he set. Da Ponte himself was acutely sensitive on the question of originality. In his memoirs, the librettist recounts his rival Giambattista Casti's grudging praise of his texts for Martín y Soler's *Il burbero di buon cuore* (after Goldoni) and for *Le nozze di Figaro* (after Beaumarchais), in each case accompanied by the disclaimer '. . .but it's only a translation'.[1] Even when there was no obvious model – and already during Da Ponte's lifetime – some critics were sifting through his librettos for evidence of literary larceny. In the pamphlet *Anti-da Ponte* of 1791 the librettist is said to merit harsh justice, for crimes which included 'the many learned thefts he has committed since the beginning of his career as a theatre-poet'.[2] Later in the same brochure, in a mock trial before a host of aggrieved parties (Mozart included), Da Ponte freely admits to having 'mercilessly plundered' 'the masterworks of Metastasio', and defends his theft of the plot of *Una cosa rara* by claiming that Martín's music was no less plagiarized.[3]

The evidence Da Ponte provides, thirty years after the fact, of his feud with Casti is hardly more admissible than the imaginary testimony in the pamphlet, but there is some truth in both sources. Casti disparaged Da Ponte's 'translations' in order to emphasize the originality of his own librettos, in a genre then mired in clichés. Italian comic operas rarely explored original subject matter; thus it was perfectly normal for Mozart to '[look] through easily a hundred librettos' when setting out to write an opera buffa of his own. In adapting and translating various plays and librettos, Da Ponte was only fulfilling duties expected of him as house poet for the Italian opera company – a position to which Casti aspired. As for literary theft, Casti was hardly any less guilty than his rival. He made a point of parading his literary learning in his opera texts, whether in outright quotations, Dantesque or Petrachan locutions, or in 'reminiscences' of recent operas.[4] Early in *Così*, when Da Ponte has Ferrando and Guglielmo characterize Alfonso's quotation of Metastasio as 'poetic nonsense' and 'old men's foolishness', he is probably mocking Casti's as much as his own erudition.

If Da Ponte's contemporaries questioned his originality largely out of malice, later generations' interest in the sources of *Così* sprang from a desire to distance Mozart from a plot generally seen as unworthy of his genius. Recent scholars have approached the search most fruitfully when they have allowed for the possibility of multiple sources. Da Ponte's epicurean approach is illustrated by his 1789 pasticcio *L'ape musicale* (The musical bee), in which the future Fiordiligi sang a retexted cavatina from Salieri's *Axur* (III/5) which explained the premise:

> Com' Ape ingegnosa
>   Sui lucidi albori
>   Dai teneri fiori
>   Sa il mele succhiar.
> Così da un tesoro
>   Di musiche note
>   Coll'arte si puote
>   Il meglio cavar.

> (As the ingenious bee sucks the honey from tender flowers upon bright trees, so can one artfully extract the best from a treasury of musical notes.)

One does well also to distinguish between proximate sources, and more peripheral themes or opinions that were simply 'in the air'. Date is not necessarily a deciding factor: the works of Virgil, Dante or Petrarch would have been more proximate, in terms of Da Ponte's knowledge and interests, than many a contemporary German play.

Myths and morals

That mythology was a fundamental source for *Così fan tutte* is suggested by the frequency with which the opera's characters invoke the pantheon of ancient deities and their stories, from Alfonso's scoffing reference to the officers' 'Penelopes' in the first scene through Guglielmo's talk of Charon's boat, shortly before the second-act finale. In a short study published in 1954, Ernst Gombrich proposed the myth of Cephalus and Procris as an archetype for *Così*, and this has stimulated much further research.[5] The Cephalus story, as related in the seventh book of Ovid's *Metamorphoses*,[6] concerns an Athenian prince who is goaded into testing the fidelity of his wife. An important difference from *Così* is the fact that Cephalus is the first to stray – though he later protests that 'Procris was in my heart, Procris was ever on my lips.' But the similarities, too, are striking. Cephalus is able to woo his own spouse because his seductress, the goddess Aurora, had changed his features; Ferrando and Guglielmo's less magical metamorphosis into Albanians affords them anonymity which they use for similar purposes, after likewise pretending to leave on a voyage. Like the officers, Cephalus repents of the test as soon as it has produced the feared result.

The myth of Cephalus and Procris was elaborated by many subsequent writers, including both Boccaccio (*De claris mulieribus*) and Ariosto.[7] But a second major theme in *Così*, that of the wager, is exemplified in the second *giornata* of Boccaccio's *Decameron*, and in Shakespeare's play *Cymbeline*, which partly derives from it. Boccaccio's *novella* – certainly a more proximate source as far as Da Ponte was concerned – begins with speculation by Bernabò Lomellin of Genoa and several other Italian merchants about their wives' behaviour during their stay in Paris. The first to speak echoes Cephalus in saying that he sees no conflict between the love he holds for his wife, and carnal pleasures taken elsewhere. Most in the group assume that their wives back home are no more celibate than they are. Only Bernabò dissents, thereby attracting the ridicule of his comrade Ambruogiuolo of Piacenza, who reminds Bernabò that 'tu medesimo di' che la moglie tua è femina e ch'ella è di carne e d'ossa come son l'altre' (. . .you yourself say that your wife is a woman and that she is of flesh and blood like the rest). This anticipates language used by Alfonso in the opening scene of *Così*, as he asks if his friends' fiancées are made of 'carne, ossa, e pelle', and proposes to test whether they are truly 'come l'altre sono'. In Boccaccio's tale it is not the doubter, but the husband, who proposes the bet to see if Ambruogiuolo can seduce his wife Zinevra. Yet it is clearly the merchant from Piacenza who pushes the issue, with long-winded, pedantic arguments to which Bernabò can only respond, colloquially, 'Io son mercatante e non fisofolo' (I'm a merchant and not a philosopher). Arriving in Genoa, Ambruogiuolo soon despairs of actually seducing Zinevra, but manages to bribe her servant (as Alfonso does Despina), thereby acquiring proofs sufficient to convince Bernabò that he had been intimate with Zinevra. In the end it is Zinevra who removes her disguise and confounds both spouse and would-be seducer, rather than the other way around. But there is something almost Mozartian (or Da Pontean) in the ending, as the offended wife forgives her husband, though he be 'mal degno'. And the proverb quoted by the narrator Filomena at the beginning of the tale: '. . .lo 'ngannatore rimane a piè dello, 'ngannato' (roughly: the deceiver ends up as the deceived) is much the same as the explanation Alfonso offers the outraged Ferrarese sisters for his part in the charade: 'V'ingannai, ma fu l'inganno / Disinganno ai vostri amanti' (I deceived you, but the deception was undeceiving for your lovers).

Così fan tutte as Ariostan capriccio

Whereas mythology remained the principal source of opera plots in eighteenth-century France, most opere serie were based on ancient history. When more fanciful material was desired, Italian librettists often turned to a pair of Renaissance epics: Torquato Tasso's *Gerusalemme liberata* and Ludovico Ariosto's *Orlando furioso*, each of which contained a wealth of attractive tales. Tim Carter has catalogued close to a hundred operas deriving from each source.[8] Two Viennese works which might be added to the list of Orlando operas are Casti's *Orlando furioso* (which remained unset), and Da Ponte's *Così fan tutte* – for one of the many reworkings of the Cephalus myth is to be found in Canto 43 of Ariosto's epic.

Despite transposition of the action to the Age of Chivalry, most elements of the Cephalus myth remain as in Ovid. Here the cuckold is a Mantuan knight who at this point in the poem is acting as host to Rinaldo. The sorceress Melissa here plays Aurora to the knight's Cephalus, suggesting (as would Alfonso) that his total faith in his wife's fidelity is premature:

Ma che ti sia fedel, tu non puoi dire,	But canst thou know thy consort's truth (she cry'd)
prima che di sua fé prova non vedi.	Till such by ample proof be fairly try'd?

(*Orlando furioso*, 43:25)

Qual prova avete voi, che ognor costanti
Vi sien le vostri amanti. . .?

(*Così fan tutte*, I/1: What proof do you have, that your lovers
are still faithful to you?)[9]

As had Ovid's Aurora, Melissa magically transforms the husband's
appearance so that he might secretly court his wife. The few lines in
which the wife's reactions are recorded (43:38) predict the women's
progression across the two acts of *Così* from outrage (Nos. 13, 14)
to hesitant interest (first finale, No. 20) to rationalization (II/2
onward) to capitulation (Nos. 23, 29). The similarities between *Così*
and this telling of the story are about as close as to Ovid's version.
But Da Ponte also borrowed some key elements from Ariosto's
frame for the tale, clearly marking *Orlando furioso* as a more direct
source for his text. The Mantuan knight recounts the destruction of
his marriage, through his own curiosity, in the context of his
proposal to test the fidelity of his guests' wives by means of a magic
cup given him by Melissa:

Chi la moglie ha pudica, bee con quello:	He freely drinks, whose consort merits praise;
ma non vi può già ber chi l' ha puttana;	Whose wife is false in vain the draught essays:
che 'l vin, quando lo crede in bocca porre,	When to the vessel's brim his lips are prest,
tutto si sparge, e fuor nel petto scorre.	The wine o'erflows and trickles down his breast.
(*Orlando furioso*, 43:28)	

In raising the goblet, the Mantuan host seemed rather to weep than
to smile, Ariosto says – an opposition appropriated and repeated by
Da Ponte. Rinaldo hesitates to drink, saying

. . .Ben sarebbe folle	. . .Insensate is the mind
chi quel che non vorria trovar, cercasse.	Who seeks for that it ne'er would wish to find.
Mia donna è donna, et ogni donna è molle:	My wife's a woman – all the sex is frail –
lasciàn star mia credenza come stasse.	But let not hence my good opinion fail:
(*Orlando furioso*, 43:6)	

Addressing his young friends, Alfonso paraphrases this warning in
the first number of Mozart's opera. In the dénouement, the officers

foreswear further tests – symmetrically bringing the plot to closure, just as Rinaldo had repeated the moral at the end of the Mantuan knight's sad tale (43:47).

The evidence for a largely Ariostan origin for *Così fan tutte* is also circumstantial. Long ago Edward Dent noted that Marcellina's aria 'Il capro e la capretta' in the fourth act of *Le nozze di Figaro* is a close imitation of the opening of Canto 5 in *Orlando furioso*, an indictment of man as the only creature that mistreats the female of its species.[10] Da Ponte's text for *Il finto cieco*, performed that same year (1786), likewise contains a reference to a character from this epic, the valorous Marfisa (I/5). Finally, Da Ponte left ample evidence, quite apart from his opera texts, of his affection for Ariosto. Near the beginning of his memoirs he calls Dante, Petrarch, Ariosto and Tasso his 'first masters', whose works he had largely committed to memory.[11] Throughout his memoirs, names from *Orlando furioso* are applied to himself and to his friends and lovers, and during his sojourn in London he even published an expurgated edition of the poem.[12] Several stanzas from Ariosto's epic were recited at 'the first Literary Conversazione, held at his house, in New-York, on the 10th of March, 1807', and no doubt on many other occasions. Da Ponte's was a life spent in constant communication with Ariosto, and the rest of the Italian literary Parnassus.

Dunstan reminds us that the Mantuan knight's tale is only the first of two stories of sexual jealousy in the forty-third Canto; the second is told to Rinaldo by the Mantuan knight's boatman, as the two make their way down the river Po.[13] Reflecting on the previous evening's test of the cup, Rinaldo avows that there would be little to be gained, and much to be lost by drinking (43:66). Helping confirm him in this belief, the boatman tells him of the insanely jealous Mantuan judge Anselmo and his clever, beautiful, but ultimately unfaithful wife Argia. The intrigue is less like that of *Così* than is the previous tale's – though Dunstan calls attention to similarities between Argia's bribable wet-nurse and Da Ponte's Despina. In the end, Argia's adultery is discovered, and in his rage Anselmo plots her murder. This fails, and with both parties chastened, the only path to a reconciliation is through oblivion:

e sia la pace e sia l'accordo fatto,	. . .henceforth let us live
ch'ogni passato error vada in oblio;	In lasting peace, and all the past forgive:
né ch'in parole io possa mai né in atto	In word or deed I ne'er will more repine

| ricordarti il tuo error, né a me tu il mio. – | At thy offence, nor shalt thou censure mine. |

(*Orlando furioso*, 43:143)

Similar sentiments are voiced – with somewhat analogous intent – in the toast to oblivion sung by the realigned lovers in the opera's second finale.

> E nel tuo, nel mio bicchiero
> Si sommerga ogni pensiero,
> E non resti più memoria
> Del passato ai nostri cor.
>
> (*Così fan tutte*, No. 31: And let every thought be submerged in your, in my glass, and let there remain in our hearts no memory of the past.)

These two tales from Canto 43 demonstrate quite diverse consequences of adultery. In the first, the disguised husband's temptation of his wife precludes any chance for happiness, while in the second, Argia's faithlessness is seen as no worse than Anselmo's maniacal jealousy, and a reconciliation ensues.

Earlier in *Orlando furioso*, in Canto 28, there is another tale of cuckoldry which, like the two such stories in Canto 43, Da Ponte suppressed in his edition of the poem.[14] Ariosto himself gives the cue, in an opening apostrophe to 'Donne, e voi che le donne avete in pregio' (Ye dames! and ye to whom each dame is dear), advising them to skip over this defamatory tale. Da Ponte mined these verses in composing 'Donne mie, la fate a tanti' (No. 26), in which Guglielmo apologizes in advance for his complaints about women's wiles. The story of Astolfo and Iocondo in Canto 28 provided another crucial element to the plot of *Così*: the doubling of the participants.[15] The famously handsome King Astolfo, curious to see the man whose fair appearance is said to rival his own, summons Iocondo to his court. The latter, after a tearful parting from his young wife, remembers that he has forgotten the necklace she had given him as a token of her love; he returns to find her in bed with a servant. Though initially appalled, Iocondo comes to see that 'Her fault was but the fault of all her kind' (28:36) – an excuse adduced also by Alfonso in No. 30 of Mozart's opera. Astolfo's own spouse soon proves equally faithless, and both vow to avenge the wrongs done them by roaming the world in disguise, seducing women. Though these two Don Juans do not court each other's partners, as in *Così*, in the end they recognize that all women are the same:

Provate mille abbiamo, e tutte belle;	A thousand women we before have try'd,
né di tante una è ancor che ne contraste.	Yet found not one our amorous suit deny'd.
Se provian l'altre, fian simili anch'elle;	A second thousand like the first would fall:
ma per ultima prova costei baste.	But this last proof may well suffice for all.
Dunque possiamo creder che più felle	Then cease we more to blame our mates, or find
non sien le nostre, o men de l'altre caste:	Their thoughts less chaste than those of all their kind;
e se son come tutte l'altre sono,	And since they both are virtuous as the best,
che torniamo a godercile fia buono.	Let us return and live with them at rest.

(*Orlando furioso*, 28:73)

The suitors in *Così fan tutte*, confronted with the choice of marrying their faithless women or remaining celibate, ask Alfonso (immediately before the second finale) if men like them would ever lack for women. He replies:

Non c'è abbondanza d'altro.	You'll find an abundance of them.
Ma l'altre, che faran, se ciò fer queste?	But what would others do, if these did this?

The humane (if not completely evenhanded) moral of the opera was thus not born of Enlightenment philosophy, but a piece of wisdom from centuries earlier.

If the portions of Ariosto's epic discussed thus far provided some essential features of Da Ponte's plot, other passages helped define the personalities of the opera's heroines. Andrew Steptoe recognized a general resemblance between Ariosto's and Da Ponte's Fiordiligis, on the one hand, and the more flighty Doralice and Dorabella on the other.[16] But Dunstan's thorough reading of Ariosto reveals both a more complicated ancestry for Dorabella, and touches of cruel parody in Da Ponte's handling of Fiordiligi. Dorabella, she writes, is not simply a version of Ariosto's Doralice, but

a composite name deriving from the two ladies who frame the story in Canto 28. Rodomonte is in love with one after the other: his fiancée Doralice betrays him for Mandricardo and Isabella escapes his embraces by cleverly contrived suicide.[17]

With Dora- -bella as precedent, Da Ponte then extracted Despina's name from that of Ariosto's Spanish princess Fiordispina.[18] And though the contexts are completely different, there is also a clear model in *Orlando furioso* (42:14) for Guglielmo's dismemberment of the name Fiordiligi (lily-flower) following her betrayal of him.[19]

Both Fiordiligi and the Saracen Isabella (or Issabella) are paragons of wifely virtue in Ariosto's poem, so when they are invoked or paraphrased in an opera called *Così fan tutte*, the effect is necessarily ironic. So devoted is Ariosto's Fiordiligi to her husband Brandimarte that he cannot bring himself to tell her of his impending departure with Orlando. When after several months he has still not returned, Fiordiligi sets off in search of him. They are eventually reunited, but when Brandimarte is killed soon afterward, Fiordiligi berates herself for not following him into combat. Thus does Da Ponte's Fiordiligi, gnawed by remorse after lending an ear to her seducer, plan to join her betrothed on the battlefield (II/11). (At this point the librettist also has Fiordiligi tear off her 'fatal' feminine ornaments, in imitation of Tasso's Rinaldo as he removes the womanish emblems of his servitude to Armida [16:31 ff.].) Fiordiligi's earlier aria 'Come scoglio', on the other hand, was apparently modelled on a speech by another faithful woman in Ariosto's epic, Ruggero's beloved Bradamante:[20]

immobil son di vera **fede scoglio**	In me behold a rock of truth, that braves
che d'ogn'intorno il **vento** e il mar percuote:	The howling tempest and the dashing waves:
né già mai per bonaccia né per verno	Not spring or winter have I chang'd my place,
luogo mutai, né muterò in eterno.	Nor aught shall ever shake my stedfast base.

(*Orlando furioso*, 44:61)

Come **scoglio immoto** resta
Contra i **venti**, e la tempesta,
Così ognor quest'alma è forte
Nella **fede**, e nell'amor. . .

(*Così fan tutte*, No. 14: As the rock remains firm against the winds and the storm, thus this soul is ever strong, in faith and in love. . .)

Da Ponte's imitation is more thoroughgoing, and in better taste, than that of Casti in *La grotta di Trofonio*, who has Plistene declare

Ma io per la mia Dori
Duro, e costante ognor, come uno scoglio.

(I/9: But for my Dori, I'm hard and ever constant, like a rock.)

Fiordiligi's reaction to the news of Bradamante's death furnished
Da Ponte with models for the hysterics of both sisters as they
contemplate life without their fiancés. Whereas the earlier Fiordiligi
merely shuns the light (43:157), before her first aria (No. 11)
Dorabella hates the light, the air she breathes, even herself.
Bradamante's widow had torn her hair and cheeks, and

. . .grida, come	
donna talor che 'l demon rio percuote,	. . .rav'd as if some fiend her soul possess'd.
o come s'ode che già a suon di corno	So seem'd the Menades, when wide were borne
Menade corse, et aggirossi intorno.	Their shouts and clamours with the maddening horn.
(*Orlando furioso*, 43:158)	

just as would Dorabella in her invocation of the Eumenides,
'Smanie implacabili'. Fiordiligi's plea for a knife to end her woes
echoes Isabella's words to her dying lover Zerbino:

Non sì tosto vedrò chiudervi gli occhi,	. . .when ruthless death shall close
o che m'ucciderà il dolore interno,	Thy fading eyes – that moment ends my woes!
o se quel non può tanto, io vi prometto	Or should I still survive that stroke of grief,
con questa spada oggi passarmi il petto.	At least thy sword will yield a sure relief.
(*Orlando furioso*, 24:81)	

Similar expressions abound in *Così fan tutte*: in the sisters' reaction
to the imminent departure of their fiancés, in No. 6 and immediately thereafter, and as their treachery is discovered in the second
finale (Andante, bb. 466 ff.). Finally, the grief-stricken Fiordiligi
shuts herself up in Brandimarte's tomb to waste away her days (see
Plate 4). When Da Ponte's Fiordiligi compares Guglielmo's absence
to death, Dorabella outdoes her, likening Ferrando's departure to
live burial (I/9). Both before and after Dorabella's fall from
innocence, Guglielmo cites the original example of such devotion,
by the Carian queen Artemisia (who had sealed herself in the tomb

CAN TO XLIII.

I.B.Cipriani del.   F.Bartolozzi Sculp.

Stava ella nel fepolcro; e quivi attrita
Da penitenza, orando giorno e notte.

Canto XLIII.Stanza CLXXXV.

4 Ariosto's Fiordiligi: engraving by F. Bartolozzi after G. B. Cipriani,
from John Baskerville's edition of *Orlando furioso* (Birmingham, 1773)

of her husband Mausolus) – first naïvely (II/11), and then ironically
(II/13).

As befits a character of such mixed ancestry, Dorabella's initial
protestations of loyalty to Ferrando soon give way to interest in a
more available lover. Once Alfonso's infidel friends appear on the
scene, her behaviour is exactly parallel to that of Doralice of
Granada who, though betrothed to the warrior Rodomonte, offers
little resistance to the advances of Mandricardo.[21] Later forced to
choose between the rivals for her hand, she prefers the newer one,
and the spurned Rodomonte vents his anger in language of the sort
used throughout *Così* by Alfonso:

– Oh feminile ingegno (egli dicea),	O female sex! (he cry'd) whose worthless mind,
come ti volgi e muti facilmente,	Inconstant, shifts with every changing wind:
contrario oggetto proprio de la fede!	O faithless woman! perjur'd and unjust,
Oh infelice, oh miser chi ti crede!	Most wretched those who place in thee their trust!

(*Orlando furioso*, 27:117)

Rodomonte pays back the false Doralice in kind, transfering his
affections to the grieving Isabella. Da Ponte seems to have found
inspiration in Ariosto's proverbial description of the process:

E ben gli par dignissima Issabella,	While Isabella worthy seem'd to prove
in cui locar debba il suo amor secondo,	The peerless object of his second love;
e spenger totalmente il primo, a modo	And from his breast expunge Granada's dame,
che da l'asse si **trae chiodo con chiodo**.	As pity yields to pity, flame to flame.

(*Orlando furioso*, 28:98)

Alf.:	Or ben; se mai per consolarle un poco	Well then, if to console them a bit
	E **trar**, come diciam, **chiodo per chiodo**,	and, so to speak, drive out one nail with another,
	Tu ritrovassi il modo	you could find a way
	Da metter in lor grazia due soggetti	to put into their good graces two clever fellows. . .
	Di garbo. . .	

(*Così fan tutte*, I/10)

Two further signs of *Così*'s inspiration in Ariosto's epic remain to be mentioned. One was removed before the opera reached performance: namely, Guglielmo's comparison of himself to 'un Orlando innamorato', in the reference-saturated aria 'Rivolgete a lui lo sguardo'. The second clue is more formal: Da Ponte's use in Alfonso's No. 30 of *ottava rima*, the type of verse used by Ariosto for the whole of *Orlando furioso*.[22] The librettist delighted in such poetic artifices, which nicely complement his borrowing of themes and vocabulary from earlier authors. They are like nuggets of gold lying on the ground, inviting the observant passer-by to dig deeper.

Ultimately, Da Ponte's aim in taking so much inspiration from Ariosto's poem was not to surpass Casti's displays of erudition – though these included references to characters from the epic, in his libretto *Prima la musica e poi le parole*, for Salieri – nor even to represent the Ferrarese poet's opinions at face value. For as we have seen, Da Ponte turns nearly all the borrowed material to one purpose: proving the foolishness of trusting in women's constancy. What the librettist hoped to gain was something of the earlier poet's psychological insight, on a subject that interested him greatly. Da Ponte's more pervasive cynicism did not prevent him from retaining Ariosto's generosity when the latter says that, though women be false, one can and must still love them. *Così fan tutte* cannot be considered a true parody, since no one story (whether from *Orlando furioso* or elsewhere) is followed from start to finish. Its effect is more that of an architectural caprice, such as were painted by Da Ponte's countrymen Antonio Canaletto and Francesco Guardi. Pictures and libretto alike include clearly recognizable elements, rearranged and placed among invented ones in a pleasing and coherent whole. Though other sources contributed to the text of *Così*, Ariosto set the tone and provided the framework. In his memoirs Da Ponte tells of taking Dante as his inspiration for Mozart's *Don Giovanni*, Petrarch as a guide for Martín's *L'arbore di Diana*, and Tasso for Salieri's *Axur*.[23] In similar fashion, Ariosto stands as godfather over the composition of *Così fan tutte*.

There is one other sixteenth-century text which Alfonso quotes outright in *Così*. As the officers' boat moves away from shore, the philosopher gleefully anticipates the ease with which he will win his bet, citing for support three lines from an eclogue in Jacopo Sannazaro's pastoral novel *L'Arcadia* (published 1504); the initial quotation marks in the original libretto show that they were meant to be recognized as a quotation:

"Nel mare solca, e nell'arena semina,
"E il vago vento spera in rete accogliere
"Chi fonda sue speranze in cor di femmina.

(*Così fan tutte*, I/7: He who places his faith in women might as
well plough the waves, sow the sands, or catch the wind in nets.)

Like so much in this libretto, this passage is proverbial, which has
prompted more than one of Sannazaro's editors to suspect that still
older models lay behind it. And like the *ottava rima* of No. 30, the
verse form calls attention to itself, with its *sdrucciolo* (dactyl-ending)
hendecasyllables. In their original context, these lines are not quite
as misogynist as they seem, for they occur within a larger debate
which includes more optimistic views of love.

Da Ponte and the 'demonstration comedy': Marivaux and Beaumarchais

However much Ariosto may have contributed to the plot and language of *Così fan tutte*, it is still very much an eighteenth-century
libretto, reliant to a large degree on convention. The company of
singers who would perform the opera had quite specific expectations
concerning the vocabulary and situations appropriate to their
character-types, and a host of other matters. Nor could Da Ponte
ignore the fact that his poetic allusions and conceits would be lost
upon a good many spectators; the piece had also to appeal to the
interests and tastes of a contemporary audience. There are several
eighteenth-century writers to whom Da Ponte probably turned in
drafting his libretto for *Così fan tutte*, including two French drama-
tists who treated the theme of sexual jealousy with notable insight.

Several recent theories on the origins of *Così fan tutte* have
revolved around the works of Pierre Marivaux, the majority of
which deal with the mysteries of the human heart. Daniel Heartz
has noted numerous convergences of themes and dramatic strategies
between the French writer's comedies and the Mozart–Da Ponte
operas, and also the popularity of the former in Vienna, whether in
the original language or in translation. *Les Fausses Confidences*, in
which 'the process of falling in love is. . .observed with a kind of
clinical detachment by an older and "philosophical" type', was
performed there repeatedly, right up to the year of *Così*'s première.[24]
For Charles Rosen, Da Ponte's libretto, like Marivaux's comedies
for the Théâtre Italien, belonged to

a genre that may be called the comedy of experimental psychology, a kind of play that was quickly taken up in Italy and Germany. These are not 'thesis' plays but 'demonstration' plays: there is never anything controversial about their ideas. They demonstrate – prove by acting out – psychological ideas and 'laws' that everyone accepted. . .The interest in such a play lies chiefly in the psychological steps by which the characters move to an end known in advance: as in Marivaux' *Le Jeu de l'amour et du hasard* [1730], how a young girl disguised as a maid and a young man disguised as a valet will overcome their feelings of class and, first, become aware that they are in love and, then, openly admit it.[25]

The link with this play was followed up by Andrew Steptoe, with particular attention to the symmetry that its plot shares with that of *Così*.[26] The element of class plays no such role for Da Ponte's crossed pairs of fiancés, but the controlling figure of Orgon does have an equivalent in Alfonso. An even more clinical experimenter is the Prince of the play *La Dispute* (1744), which Nicholas Till has recently proposed as the principal model for *Così*.[27] The dispute of the title concerned the question: Which sex is more inconstant in love? To settle the matter, the Prince's father had ordered two pairs of children to be raised in isolation; when a bet is made on the same issue nearly two decades later, the son sets the demonstration in motion. The two couples go into raptures upon first meeting, but when the females are exposed to their opposite numbers from the other pair, they trade partners with little ado. As in Da Ponte's plot, the tokens of betrayal are portraits, and in the end the original couples are rejoined. But, as one of the observers complains, this dénouement is due merely to the male sex's propensity to change 'for no reason, without even seeking an excuse' (Scene 20) – a notion far removed from the moral of *Così*, or of the tale of Astolfo and Iocondo.

The original production of *La Dispute* was a failure, but the curious could still read it in editions of Marivaux's works. In 1778 Marivaux's play was translated by Johann Friedrich Schmidt, and published in Vienna as *Wer ist in der Liebe unbeständig?*, in a volume of prize-winning plays for the new Nationaltheater.[28] That same year it was adapted by Johann Josef Kurz as a Singspiel, and performed in the Burgtheater with music by Franz Aspelmayr, under the title *Die Kinder der Natur*. It is conceivable that, in one form or another, the play could have come to Mozart's attention; if Da Ponte encountered the work, it would probably have been in the original language. Was *La Dispute* 'the' source for *Così fan tutte*? A comparison of the language of the two pieces suggests that it was not. The young lovers in *La Dispute*, innocent of any sort of moral code, speak with a naïveté reminiscent of Favart, whereas the fiancés of *Così* start from very fixed, though unrealistic, notions of fidelity and honour. In terms of the mechanics of the plot, Da Ponte needed to look no farther than the garden scene of his own *Le nozze di Figaro* to find an example of crossed pairs of lovers. *Così fan tutte* relates to *La Dispute* and other comedies by Marivaux simply as an example of a widespread type. It is rather in their portrayals of women gradually becoming aware of love, or struggling against it (as in Fiordiligi's anguished *rondò*) that Da Ponte and Marivaux intersect most closely.

Throughout his libretto, Da Ponte rang changes on the title *Così fan tutte*, just as Beaumarchais had burned the theme of jealousy into the minds of the spectators in his earlier play *Le Barbier de Séville* through repeated statements of its subtitle, *La Précaution inutile*. Mozart's collaborator may also have taken a hint from Beaumarchais when he had Ferrando taunt the freshly betrayed Guglielmo with his own earlier boasts ('Un poco di più merto. . .'), for there is just such a scene in the fourth act of *Le Mariage de Figaro*, in which Marceline throws Figaro's sanguine philosophy on jealousy back in his face after he has learnt of Suzanne's assignation with the Count.

In a sense, *Così fan tutte*, *Il barbiere di Siviglia* and *Fra i due litiganti il terzo gode* (after Goldoni) are all 'demonstration comedies', in that their titles or subtitles foretell the outcome of the drama. *Così fan tutte* also bears a relation – in rather a roundabout way – to another subgenre of eighteenth-century drama: sentimental comedy. Its plot is based on the officers' sentimental conviction that their women are superior beings, and on their fiancées' pity for the mysterious 'strangers', which is manipulated into something that they mistake for love. In addition, the text displays some of what Frank Ellis has termed the 'secondary characteristics' of sentimental comedy: undeserved distress (the sisters', following the departure of their men); reckless, self-sacrificing virtue (the fiancées' hysterics, and particularly Fiordiligi's decision to follow Guglielmo to the battle-ground); and a great deal of overt moralizing.[29] Of course most of the sentimentality is included in order to be mocked or contradicted – as in Alfonso's scoffing dismissal of 'tears, sighs, caresses, swooning' (I/1). By the start of the second finale, all the lovers are more or less converted to the anti-sentimental position of Alfonso and Despina. But this conversion is not sufficiently reflective for the opera simply to end with the marriage of the new couples. The rules of comedy require that the 'distress-providing' characters unmask and reveal their 'essential good nature', and that the (original) lovers confess and renounce their faults in full knowledge of their situation, so they may be free to enjoy one another.[30] Da Ponte varies the formula in interesting ways. Alfonso wears his disguise by proxy, in that the good purpose of his scheme is revealed only by the soldiers' unmasking. Despina, after removing her notary's costume, remains perplexed by the dénouement, as Alfonso had revealed only a part of his design to her. Mozart's music frequently seems to encourage the lovers' illusions, perhaps more than Da Ponte had envisaged. The text's constant invitations to operatic parody determined his approach in many instances – though not to the exclusion of heartfelt sentiment.

Opera out of opera.

Of the operatic prototypes for the text of *Così fan tutte*, the first to claim our attention, Goldoni's *Le pescatrici* (The fisherwomen), comes from an earlier efflorescence of opera buffa in the Burgtheater, before Joseph II's experiment with a *Nationalsingspiel*. The opera was performed in Vienna in 1771, with music by Florian Gassmann, and pleased Joseph so much that he sent copies of its libretto and score to his brother Leopold in Florence.[31] Whether its libretto was among those examined by Da Ponte on his arrival in the capital, we cannot say, but it is probable that he knew the work, in whose third act one finds the plot and characters of *Così* prefigured.[32] After the conclusion of the opera's main action, the fishermen Burlotto and Frisellino, in love with each other's sisters, decide to test the fidelity of their girlfriends. They borrow fine clothes and moustaches and, disguised as noblemen, offer to take Nerina and Lesbina away with them to a better fate. (They do not reverse the original pairing, as this would be double incest.) When the women quickly agree to the proposition, the men remove their costumes, with ironic *révérences* such as the unmasked Ferrando would make to his 'bella damina'. The wise old fisherman Mastriccio comes upon the couples, and hearing the nature of their dispute, berates his foolish young friends for tempting fate. His solution – marriage, and silence on the past – is the one proposed by Alfonso:

E chi, pazzi, v'insegna
Le femmine tentare? In caso tale
Che avreste fatto voi, sciocchi che siete?
Se bene a lor volete,
Sposatele, tacete, e non parlate:
Si strapperà, se troppo la tirate.
. . . .
Chi va il male cercando, il mal ritrova.

(Goldoni, *Le pescatrici*, III/7: And who taught you idiots to go
tempting women? What might you have done in a similar case,
fools that you are? If you wish them well, marry them, be
silent, and say nothing; what is drawn too tight will snap. . .He
who goes looking for trouble will find it.)

These lines suggest that Goldoni, too, was well acquainted with
Orlando furioso, and Canto 43 in particular. But the passage in
question occupies a mere handful of pages in *Le pescatrici*; even if
Da Ponte did borrow the premise or other details from his coun-
tryman's earlier opera, he could not have crafted the libretto he did
without independent recourse to Ariosto.

Despite frequent reminders (allusions to *cicisbei*,[33] to Mesmer)
that we are in the eighteenth century, *Così fan tutte* has a timeless
quality which stems in part from Alfonso's reliance on proverbs.
The first of these brings together several layers of Da Ponte's source
material. Amused by Ferrando and Guglielmo's innocent faith in
the constancy of their fiancées, Alfonso adduces an old saying:

È la fede delle femmine
Come l'araba fenice:
Che vi sia, ciascun lo dice;
Dove sia. . .nessun lo sa.

(*Così fan tutte*, No. 2: The faith of women is like the Arabian
phoenix; everyone says it exists, but no one knows where to
find it.)

Many in the audience would have recognized the quatrain as
coming from Metastasio's *Demetrio* of 1731, which was set by more
than fifty composers over the next century. Guglielmo and Ferrando
certainly do, judging from their reactions. Da Ponte's intent is not in
the main parodistic; in his memoirs he recalled how on first encoun-
tering them, Metastasio's 'verses produced the same sensation in my
soul as does music'.[34] Metastasio's phoenix stands as a harbinger of
much opera seria language to come, notably in Ferrando's second

aria, whose Metastasian ancestry has already already been mentioned (see Synopsis). Even if a spectator was unacquainted with opera seria, he might recognize Alfonso's lines in the second terzetto from canonic settings of them by Metastasio himself (published in 1782), and by Martín (published 1787). (In these versions, as in *Demetrio*, the first line ends more impartially with 'amanti'.) The writing of canons, often on scurrilous texts, had long been a pastime of composers; in Josephinian Vienna it spilt over onto the stage, with the inclusion of canons in both *L'arbore di Diana* and *Una cosa rara* by Martín, in Salieri's *Axur* (1788), and Mozart's sublime canon in the second finale of *Così*.[35]

The lineage of Alfonso's borrowed quatrain extends further in both directions. The phoenix was ubiquitous in literature as an image of the myth of female constancy, though the Mozartian singer Michael Kelly identified its original author as St Jerome.[36] The metaphor occurs also in the frame to the tale of Astolfo and Iocondo (27:136). Daniel Heartz has observed that 'Da Ponte was not the first comic librettist to cite this particular verse [from *Demetrio*]. Goldoni used it in *La scuola moderna* (1748), and in a manner that made clear it was a borrowing.'[37] Da Ponte himself reused it in an opera for London, *L'isola del piacere* (1795, with music by Martín).[38] And at the time he wrote *Così fan tutte*, Da Ponte had used the phoenix metaphor twice already, in his librettos for *Il ricco d'un giorno* (1784) and *Una cosa rara* (1786). As employed in the former work, the derivation from Metastasio is particularly clear:

Giacinto: Siete savissima,
               Ciascun lo dice,
               Siete l'arabica
               Rara Fenice. . .

               (*Il ricco d'un giorno*, II/9: You are most wise, everyone says
               it, you are the rare Arabian phoenix. . .)

For spectators at performances of *Così*, then, Alfonso's quotation would have resonated in any number of ways, depending on the breadth of their reading and theatrical experiences.

Two Da Pontean librettos from 1786 offer such striking similarities to scenes in *Così fan tutte* that one can assume that the poet had consciously mined them for useful material. In *Il finto cieco* the protagonist Sempronio (whose name would serve as Ferrando's

Albanian pseudonym) sings an aria text uncannily close to that of
the opening trio of *Così* in its premise, setting and use of Latin:

> Vidi una volta – Certi filosofi,
> Che disputavano – Dentro un caffè.
> Uno gridava – *Infida est foemmina.*
> L'altro strillava – *Infidus masculus.* . .
>
> (Da Ponte/Gazzaniga, *Il finto cieco*, I/11: Once I saw certain
> philosophers arguing in a café. One cried 'Women are faithless.'
> The other screamed 'Faithless is man'. . .)

Significantly, the dispute ends in a draw. Parallels to *Così* are no less
evident in *Una cosa rara*, where Lilla and Ghita's discussion of how
love need not enter into certain types of amorous arrangements
foreshadows the scenes in Act II in which Fiordiligi, Dorabella and
Despina debate the morality of a 'diversion' with the Albanian
suitors. Ghita's subsequent aria 'Colla flemma che tu vedi' is
extremely close to Despina's 'Una donna a quindici anni', as regards
both content and form; the pieces' musical similarities will occupy
us further in Chapter 6. There are reminiscences in *Così* also of Da
Ponte's *L'arbore di Diana*. Besides the theme of inevitable capitulation to love, there is a precedent (in Britomarte's aria 'De' tre, che
qui veggio') for Fiordiligi and Dorabella's choosing of lovers according to hair colour, in their duet 'Prenderò quel brunettino'. And as
Dorothea Link has pointed out, for members of the original
audience of *Così*, Dorabella's aria 'È Amore un ladroncello' would
have brought to mind not just 'love' or 'Cupid', but also Louise
Villeneuve, the singer of Amore in the earlier opera, and the
Dorabella of *Così*.[39] Indeed, the aria Dorabella sings in order to
justify her behaviour provides an ironic contrast to the words of
Amore's third aria in *L'arbore di Diana*:

> Si dice qua e là
> Amore è un bricconcello,
> Che intorbida il cervello,
> Che sospirar ci fa.
>
> Nessun lo crede già!
> Amore è buono e bello,
> Amore è solo quello
> Che dà felicità.
>
> (*L'arbore di Diana*, I/11: It is said here and there that Cupid is
> a rascal who muddles our brains, who makes us sigh. Don't

anyone believe it! Cupid is good and fair, it is Cupid alone who gives happiness.)

È Amore un ladroncello,
Un serpentello è Amore;
Ei toglie e dà la pace,
Come gli piace, ai cor. . .

(*Così fan tutte*, No. 28: Cupid is a little thief, Cupid is a little snake; he gives and takes our hearts' peace, as it pleases him. . .)

The fact that Dorabella's aria was a late addition to the score suggests all the more strongly that Mozart intended the piece as a comment on the aria in Martín's opera, which was still in the repertory.

It was natural enough for Da Ponte to allude to passages from his own previous works; between his librettos and those of his rival Casti there is a rather more uneasy relationship. Even if Da Ponte occasionally found inspiration in his competitor's works, another concern was to avenge Casti's slanderous portrayal of him in his libretto to Salieri's *Prima la musica e poi le parole*, and to achieve the sort of success Casti had scored with the Viennese public with his and Paisiello's *Il re Teodoro in Venezia*. In his memoirs Da Ponte complains that following the opera's première in 1784 Casti was considered well nigh as 'infallible in Vienna as the Pope in Rome',[40] and enumerates the libretto's many shortcomings. The poet was also the subject of Da Ponte's satirical poem 'Epistola all'Abate Casti', published in 1786. In some respects, Da Ponte's text for *Così fan tutte* can also be considered as a response to Casti. The noisy *chiusa* first finale of *Il re Teodoro*:

Che sussurro! che bisbilio
Or mi ronza nell'orecchio.
Non rimiro ovunque volgomi[;]
Che disordine, e scompiglio. . .

(*Il re Teodoro in Venezia*, Finale I: What a racket! what noise is buzzing in my ear! I don't know where to turn; what disorder and confusion!)

is seemingly echoed in the exaggerated protests of the offended sisters in No. 13 of *Così*. At the conclusion of this piece, which prematurely exhibits the form and cacophony of a finale, Alfonso enters asking.

Che sussurro, che strepito,
Che scompiglio è mai questo,
Siete pazze care le mie ragazze,
Volete solevar il vicinato,
Cos'avete, ch'è nato?

(*Così fan tutte*, No. 13: What is this noise, this racket, whatever
is all this confusion? Are you mad, my dear girls, do you wish
to rouse the neighbourhood? What's the matter, what has
happened?)

Da Ponte faulted Casti also for the 'unlikely and almost tragic'
ending of his opera,[41] in which the king narrowly escapes debtor's
prison. In Teodoro's reflections on the caprices of fortune we see a
rather repetitive antecedent of Alfonso's philosophical lesson at the
end of *Così*:

Come una ruota è il mondo,
    Chi in cima sta, chi in fondo,
    E chi era in fondo prima,
    Poscia ritorna in cima,
    Chi salta, che precipita
    E chi va in sù, chi in giù.
Ma se la ruota gira,
    Lascisi pur girar,
Felice è chi fra i vortici
    Tranquillo può restar.

(*Il re Teodoro in Venezia*, II/20: The world is like a wheel; now
some are at the summit, some at the bottom, and he who at
first was on the bottom later returns to the summit; some leap
up, some tumble, and some go up, some go down. But if the
wheel turns, let it turn; happy is he who can remain calm
among the vortices.)

Casti's *La grotta di Trofonio* also comes in for criticism in Da
Ponte's memoirs, and though Edward Dent and others have called
the work a model for *Così fan tutte*, this is at best only superficially
true. Casti's plot resembles Da Ponte's in that it features two pairs
of lovers who are are manipulated by a 'philosopher', Trofonio. But
in the serious couple's discussion of marriage in their first-act duet
one sees that fidelity is by no means assumed, as at the equivalent
point in *Così*. In Casti and Salieri's opera there is no wager, no test
of fidelity, not even the suggestion that the partners will be
exchanged. Trofonio is really more of a sorcerer than a philosopher;
it is the bookish Ofelia and her sober Artemidore who represent the

latter occupation – through continual talk of 'reading, retirement and quiet', and the carrying around of volumes of Plato. After several repetitious transformations of character, as they enter and emerge from Trofonio's cave, the lovers are restored to their original states – having learnt nothing, and the opera ends with no moral whatsoever. One can easily imagine Da Ponte thinking how much more might be done with such a premise. And indeed, in *Così fan tutte* Alfonso teaches a truer sort of philosophy, summed up by all in terms reminiscent of the moral of *Il re Teodoro* (though more succinctly), and of Plistene's advice (in *Trofonio*) about taking marriage the right way ('pel buon verso'):

> Fortunato l'uom che prende
> Ogni cosa pel buon verso
> E tra i casi e le vicende
> Da ragion guidar si fa.
> Quel che suole altrui far piangere
> Fia per lui cagion di riso
> E del mondo in mezzo i turbini
> Bella calma troverà.

> (*Così fan tutte*, No. 31: Fortunate is the man who looks at all things on the bright side, and in all cases and through every vicissitude lets himself be guided by reason. That which is wont to make others weep is for him a cause for laughter, and amid the storms and whirlwinds of the world he will find perfect calm.)

Looking beyond Casti to other librettists' works for the Viennese opera buffa company, two operas from the first season of 1783 invite comparison to *Così*. The very first piece presented by the troupe was Salieri's *La scuola de' gelosi* (Venice, 1778), on a text by Da Ponte's former mentor Caterino Mazzolà. Here a lieutenant plays a part analogous to that of Don Alfonso in *Così*, dispassionately manipulating the partners in two couples disrupted by jealousy and illicit lust, in order to effect a reconciliation.[42] The strategy was hardly new (Rousseau uses it in *Le Devin du village*), but the assortment of characters in the piece and its title do suggest a connection. Even closer to *Così*'s plot is that of Pasquale Anfossi's *Il curioso indiscreto*, originally written for Rome in 1777 (by either Giovanni Bertati or Giuseppe Petrosellini), for which Mozart reset several numbers when the opera was given in Vienna. The story is based on an episode from Cervantes's *Don Quixote*, in which elements from both the Cephalus myth and Ariosto's tale of the Mantuan knight are already mixed. A Marchese Calandrino seeks to test the fidelity of his fiancée, by having his friend the Contino woo her, with the result that the latter two fall in love. The Contino is initially reluctant to do the Marchese's bidding, saying

> Ma questo, perdonate,
> È andar cercando il mal. . .
>
> (But this, pardon my saying so, is looking for trouble. . .)

to which Calandrino responds, 'I am only seeking my peace of mind.' It is hard to imagine that Da Ponte did not at least recall these lines when drafting his libretto to *Così*, whether or not *Il curioso indiscreto* had prompted him to explore the same subject matter.

Looking still further afield, one encounters other operatic traditions which Da Ponte may well have had in mind as he shaped his libretto. One of these was the custom whereby (according to Goldoni) the soubrette of an Italian opera buffa troupe gave 'several times every year pieces which were called transformations. . .in which the actress, appearing under different forms, was obliged to change her dress frequently, to act different characters and speak various languages'.[43] This describes precisely the nature of Despina's roles in the two finales of *Così fan tutte*. All three of Guglielmo's arias (counting the discarded 'Rivolgete') belonged to types of long standing: the self-portrait/catalogue aria or the 'women-are-fickle' aria. The latter category was particularly widespread, and included a sub-class in which 'le donne' are apostrophized directly – as also in Ariosto's introduction to Canto 28. One of the many examples of such texts by Goldoni occurs in *La mascherata* (1751), an opera so denigrating of women that the poet felt obliged to balance it with another, *Le donne vendicate* (Women avenged). Da Ponte and Mozart had similar concerns about alienating female spectators, and so included an aria ('In uomini, in soldati') in which Despina upbraids men at least as mercilessly as Guglielmo does women.

Once Da Ponte had decided what source material to use and what to reject, and drafted a text which corresponded to the norms of opera buffa practice, it was still far from being a finished libretto. Mozart invariably asked his poets for changes, additions and cuts, in the interests of effective musical theatre. Scant evidence remains of this process with regard to *Così* – apart from the changes in the first scene, compared to the version set by Salieri. But we can be sure that it included discussion of the numerous literary allusions Da Ponte had included in his text. As the composer had once declared that a comic opera was no place for anything 'learned' (gelehrtes),[44] it is likely that Da Ponte had to convince him of the comic or moral value of a good many of his quotations and paraphrases of earlier poets. An illuminating example of accommodation is provided by the Latin greeting sung to the sisters by Despina-as-notary, which is correct in Da Ponte's libretto, but comically garbled ('Salvete amabiles / Bones puelles') in Mozart's score. That poet and composer were able to arrive at something approaching a common purpose in *Così fan tutte* is suggested also by the fact that in this opera, as in their previous collaborations, Mozart put aside his stated aversion to prominent rhymes, giving free rein to Da Ponte's virtuoso talent in this sphere. The librettist, too, must have yielded on some points, or at least watched in wonder as his literary conceits and strokes of high comedy acquired new and deeper meanings, in the garb of Mozart's sublime music.

5 Così fan tutte, or 'La Partie carrée': the eighteenth-century context of a theatrical subject

The privilege of enjoying stage works long after the eras that produced them comes at a considerable cost. As historical artefacts, they can never be as fresh to a modern public as they were to one contemporary with their creation. An audience's comprehension – and consequently enjoyment – suffer not only when vocabulary or concepts treated in an old play or opera are lost to history, but also when they survive with definitions or connotations that have evolved through time. The gradual winnowing of the theatrical repertory also distorts the picture: we attribute unique value to surviving pieces, or features of them, which may or may not be representative of their times. In an effort to gain some perspective on *Così fan tutte* – a most intriguing and disturbing survivor from the Viennese opera buffa repertory, in Chapter 4 we surveyed some of the more proximate sources on which its librettist likely drew. One might easily expand the circle outwards to include any number of plays satirizing Mesmerism, operas featuring exchanges of partners, or even works concerning the relations of soldiers and women.[1] (J. M. R. Lenz's *Die Soldaten* of 1775 presents an especially grim picture of the latter subject matter, with a remorseless realism that stands in considerable contrast to the artificiality of Da Ponte's *Così*.) In the present chapter we will examine a fairly small number of contemporary writings, chosen for the light they shed on the question of how the society of 1790s Vienna (and of the 'republic of letters') might have fitted *Così fan tutte* into its moral and philosophical universe.

Philosophers and *philosophes*

In describing his several productions of *Così fan tutte*, director Jonathan Miller has dismissed the usual presentation of Don Alfonso as an 'old cynic'.

82

I have always seen him as a genuine eighteenth-century philosopher, a mixture of Diderot and Voltaire, and this means that the opera then becomes an experiment with human nature. In the first scene, to show him as a philosopher and not a joker, I had him appear at a table covered with books and classical references – the drawings of Sir William Hamilton's Neapolitan Collections, some of Galvani's early experiments on animal electricity, and there might be a mesmeric tub in his room. He is interested in all these scientific and intellectual developments of the Enlightenment. The view that ultimately all human beings are the same because all individuals partake in the nature of Man is an eighteenth-century idea. It follows that if there is any escape from a basic human nature it is achieved only by acknowledging those parts of oneself that cannot be altered.[2]

There is much in the libretto to support such an interpretation, even if Alfonso does often sugar the pill of his lessons with humour. He speaks explicitly of proofs and experimentation (II/9: 'Vo che facciamo qualche altra esperienza'), and his comments on the inevitability and unpredictability of desire, regardless of any vows, have counterparts in the writings of several eighteenth-century *philosophes* (see below). But Miller's portrayal of Alfonso as an experimental social-scientist makes both too much and too little of his part in the drama. Though it is from him that the officers await their orders in the charade, Despina is the actual instigator of the Mesmerian cure:

Alf.:   E come far vuoi perchè ritornino
            Or che partiti sono, e che li sentano
            E tentare si lascino
            Queste tue bestioline?
Des.:   A me lasciate
            La briga di condur tutta la macchina.

(I/13: *Alf.:* And how do you propose to make them return, now that they have gone, and to make these two creatures of yours hear and be tempted by them? *Des.:* Leave to me the trouble of conducting the whole plot.)

At the same time, Miller's depiction leaves out other important aspects of 'philosophy', which to an eighteenth-century audience would have been just as evident in the character of Alfonso.

In Da Ponte's time the term 'philosopher' did not always have the same scientific or academic connotations it now does. Portrayals of philosophers on the stage were varied indeed: as sage or recluse (e.g., *Il filosofo di campagna*, a *dramma giocoso* by Goldoni from 1754), as misogynist (Hilverding's ballet *Le Philosophe amoureux*, 1758),[3] as an actual Enlightenment *philosophe* (Palissot's comedy *Les Philosophes*, 1760), or as a lover disguised as an ancient Greek philosopher (Paisiello's opera *I filosofi immaginari*, 1779), to take just a few examples. The revised Richelet *Dictionnaire* of 1775 gives as its primary definition of philosophy 'love of wisdom' or 'clear and distinct knowledge of things natural and divine', but other senses of the word are given as well, including 'firmness and loftiness of mind by which one puts oneself above the accidents of life and the false opinions of the world'.[4] It is precisely this trait which so distinguishes Alfonso from his young friends, and which moves him to explain to them that '. . .in ogni cosa / Ci vuol filosofia' (philosophy is necessary in all things), after both fiancées have proven unfaithful. A 'philosophical' attitude implied a forgiving nature, as one sees at the end of *Così*, and also in an anecdote from the youth of Da Ponte's friend Giacomo Casanova, at the time newly arrived in Paris. Having just made an enormous faux pas, the embarrassed Casanova apologizes profusely. But the offended party simply laughs it off, demonstrating what Casanova called 'the practical and natural philosophy of which the French make such a noble use for the happiness of life, under the appearance of frivolity!'[5] As we have seen in Chapter 4, Da Ponte was well aquainted with the exploration of this sort of philosophy – particularly with regard to jealousy – in the works of the French playwright Beaumarchais.

Alfonso's talk of 'esperienza' connotes not only experiments, but also real life experience of the sort that had given him the 'gray hairs' of which he speaks in his first words in the opera, and in this sense too he can be called a 'philosopher'. But during the 'philosophical' eighteenth century the term 'philosopher' took on yet another meaning: 'one who by his libertine spirit places himself above the duties and obligations of civil and Christian life', according to the above-cited dictionary. Booksellers and readers alike referred to a broad category of 'livres philosophiques' encompassing works deemed politically subversive, blasphemous or pornographic in varying degrees. (Sade made the erotic connection explicit, in his *La Philosophie dans le boudoir* of 1795.) If the subject matter of *Le nozze di Figaro* and *Don Giovanni* tended towards these first two descriptions, respectively, the preliminary version of Da Ponte's libretto for *Così fan tutte* bordered on being 'philosophical' in the latter sense, with Guglielmo's mildly obscene mention of 'qualche altro capitale' in 'Rivolgete a lui lo sguardo'; even the final libretto still contained all but the last word of an obscene rhyme (see Synopsis, II/8). The conjunction in *Così* of Alfonso's talk of 'filosofia', Despina's recommendations of a libertine lifestyle, and Guglielmo's off-colour provocations made for a broad target, for those suspicious of philosophy's encroachments on traditional morality.

If we put aside for the moment the more secondary aspects of philosophy in *Così*, there remains a core of ideas on love, fidelity and enlightenment for which models can readily be found in the writings of eighteenth-century *philosophes*. The entire opera is premised on Rousseau's notion that experience precedes understanding. Alfonso cannot simply tell the soldiers that women are inconstant, or the sisters that they know precious little about love. If they are to truly learn his lessons, they must experience the pain that comes from being undeceived of their initial notions. The cruelty for which Don Alfonso has so often been criticized is the same as that of the tutor in Rousseau's *Émile, ou De l'éducation*, whose pedagogy amounts to 'a minutely organized and vigilantly executed conspiracy.'[6] His deceptions can only be revealed at a moment when his pupil is sufficiently mature and experienced to appreciate the reasons for them. As Jonathan Miller, Nicholas Till and others have noted, Alfonso seems also to know his Diderot, in whose works the promises of lovers are repeatedly mocked:

The first vows sworn by two creatures of flesh and blood were made at the foot of a rock that was crumbling to dust; they called as witness to their constancy a heaven which never stays the same for one moment; everything within them and around them was changing, and they thought their hearts were exempt from vicissitudes. Children![7]

Similarly, before her first aria Despina dismisses her mistress's talk of fidelity, saying, 'Come now! The days of telling such tales to children are past!' It is Despina, not Alfonso, who presents the most complete 'philosophy' of love in *Così fan tutte*. The creed she recites just before the first finale is a mixture of proverbial folk-wisdom and current 'naturalist' philosophy, probably learnt second-hand. The taking of a second lover, she declares, is not merely prudence, but a 'law of nature'.

> . . .amor cos'è?
> Piacer, comodo, gusto,
> Gioia, divertimento,
> Passatempo, allegria: non è più amore
> Se incomodo diventa:
> Se invece di piacer nuoce e tormenta.

> (I/13: What is love? Pleasure, convenience, taste, joy, diversion, pastime, enjoyment: it is no longer love if it becomes inconvenient, if instead of being pleasant it harms and causes pain.)

Thus would Sade declare that virtue becomes a vice when it conflicts with the laws of nature.[8] Despina picks up the thread of her casuistic discourse on love at the beginning of the next act, explaining that an infidelity is harmless if no one finds out about it.

Though Despina helps devise the patently transparent ruses of Alfonso's plot, she is also taken in by it: 'the trickster tricked', as in many a folk tradition, and numerous comic operas as well.[9] Her deep disappointment upon learning that the Albanians are in fact the original lovers, and on seeing the willingness of the sisters to return to their forgiving fiancés, demonstrates the ultimate hollowness of her libertinism. In any case, even at the height of the Josephinian liberalism, it would have been most unusual for a philosophy as licentious as hers to go unchallenged at the dénouement of a work for the stage.

The conflicting claims of passion, reason and honour on the human heart were central concerns of eighteenth-century opera, but only because these had long figured among the essential topics of European literature. At the beginning of Canto 11 of *Orlando furioso*, for instance, as Ruggero put out of mind his beloved Bradamante and pursued the more available Angelica, Ariosto had commented:

Quantunque debil freno a mezzo il corso	In mid career the rider oft restrains
animoso destrier spesso raccolga,	The fiery courser's speed with gentle reins;
raro è però che di ragione il morso	But seldom reason's curb will hold confin'd
libidinosa furia a dietro volga. . .	Th' unruly passions of an amorous mind.

Nor did writers need to await the discovery of Tahiti in order to concern themselves with the relative merits of 'civilised' and 'natural' models of love. From Antiquity through the Renaissance and beyond, the pastoral tradition is replete with dialogues in which examples from nature are adduced in support of either constancy or infidelity. Had Diderot needed a model, he could have found one close at hand in the contest of suitors – a flighty Frenchman, jealous Spaniard and 'innocent' native – in the entrée 'Les Sauvages' in Fuzelier and Rameau's *opéra-ballet Les Indes galantes* of 1735, or in the parody of it by Favart. The difference is that in *Così* the game is pursued much further, by contemporary protagonists with whom an audience could identify more readily.

Pezzl on love and Enlightenment

As a cosmopolitan city and the capital of an empire, Vienna provided a ready market for guide books describing its monuments and the customs and occupations of its inhabitants. One such guide had been published in 1770 by Joseph Weiskern, one of the leading playwrights for the city's German theatre. Another, the *Skizze von Wien* (Sketch of Vienna) by Johann Pezzl, a brother Mason from Mozart's own lodge, appeared in instalments between 1786 and 1790: precisely the same span of years of the composer's collaboration with Da Ponte. Pezzl was an enthusiastic supporter of Emperor Joseph's wide-ranging reforms; this is clear not only from comments in his *Skizze*, but also from a 'philosophical' novel he had published in 1783, a copy of which is listed in the inventory of books in Mozart's possession upon his death.[10] In the *Skizze von Wien* Pezzl is at pains to distinguish between the 'true Enlightenment', into which it was necessary to be initiated, and the 'nonsensical clamour-ings. . .during the last decade (more or less) concerning the *word* "Enlightenment"', by the hordes of writers emboldened by Joseph's easing of censorship.[11] Most of these pamphleteers had understood and digested the notions of the *philosophes* only imperfectly, and Pezzl has to admit that the larger part of the Viennese public was still at the initial stage of giving up its old prejudices. Here he is speaking mainly of the lower orders of society; aristocrats, who constituted a substantial portion of the Burgtheater audience, and who in any case were generally well-travelled, had had no difficulty in procuring the writings of the French *philosophes* even at the height of Maria Theresia's censorship.

Pezzl's discussions of love and philosophy are intertwined to a certain extent, and though optimistic elsewhere with regard to the progress of Enlightenment locally, in his chapters 'On love', 'On gallantry' and 'On marriage' he shows a cynicism nearly equal to that of Despina. The city's cultivated bachelors, he says, 'have taken as their creed in the dogma of love the oracular pronouncement of the wise Buffon.'

'O Love!' exclaims this great philosopher, 'O Love!. . .Why are you responsible for the happy condition of all beasts and the unhappiness of mankind?. . .This is so', answers the philosopher himself, 'because only the physical part of this passion is good; because the moral component. . .is good for nothing, etc.'
Who feels strong enough to contradict the great philosopher?[12]

At the beginning of the century, Pezzl relates, Viennese of all classes still fell madly in love, and until a decade or so previously (i.e. about 1775), some flickerings of such passions were still to be found in the novels of the *Sturm und Drang*; but

this paroxysm, too, is now past. In any case it was never able to take root in Vienna, or in any large city where one possessed knowledge of the world and its manners [Weltkenntnis und Lebensart].[13]

The wise modern lover, Pezzl says, moves on to a new beauty before boredom sets in. True love was not entirely dead in Vienna, he says, it was just confined to the middle and lower classes. Even the lesser nobility generally married for reasons of financial or social standing.

Since these intentions are quite open, and the bride fully realizes that matters turn not on her person, but on an important matter of secondary interest, she entertains no illusions about her husband's true affections and is in no wise disappointed in her expectations. She marries him because by doing so she can become a matron, live more easily and be mistress of the house. . .but now she has the choice of a lover who will provide compensation for her husband's bored indifference.[14]

Pezzl's representation of love and marriage in Vienna, if accurate, has possible implications for the genesis and reception of *Così fan tutte*. Da Ponte and Mozart could be fairly sure that the Burgtheater public would have quickly seen through the 'paroxysms' of the Ferrarese sisters' grief and the 'wild outbursts of passion' on the part of their suitors, and smiled knowingly as Alfonso scoffed at the lovers' 'smorfie del secolo passato'. And, to judge by Pezzl's account, the spectators would have been able to predict long before the dénouement that the original lovers would reunite.

It is incontrovertibly boring and monotonous, the way love, eternal love, is chewed over in all our comedies, and by straight and crooked paths the play always has to end in a wedding. But on top of that it is even more intolerable that all this business of love and marriage is represented in a completely false and perverted manner. The theatre should be the mirror of life: How falsely it reflects![15]

Da Ponte was perfectly aware how expected was the wedding at the end of every comedy, even playing upon this expectation in the second-act finale of *Le nozze di Figaro*:

{Sus.,   Eh via, chetati, balordo,
{Cnt.sa: La burletta ha da finir.
Fig.:   Per finirla lietamente
            E all'usanza teatrale,

Un'azion matrimoniale
Le farem ora seguir.

(*Sus., Cnt.sa:* Come now, be quiet, you blockhead, this
comedy's got to come to an end. *Fig.:* In order to finish it
happily, and according to theatrical practice, we'll proceed to
the marriage ceremony.)

But it was Da Ponte's intention in *Così fan tutte* neither merely to
retail to his audience the usual collection of clichés on love, nor to
mock them with the same wry sarcasm as does Pezzl in his *Skizze*.
Drawing on sources far older than his own century, and showing
rather more optimism than Pezzl, Da Ponte used his libretto as a
tool in the further enlightenment of his Viennese public. By showing
them the real sufferings of a Fiordiligi wracked by guilt, and the
redeeming possibility of forgiveness, he encouraged them to consider
a richer emotional existence than the sensualist lives many of them
were currently living. But the extent to which this message was the
one actually taken away by spectators was dependent also on
Mozart's music, which necessarily altered the emphases, tone and
even comprehensibility of Da Ponte's poetry.

Casanova: '. . .*così son tutte*'

Da Ponte wrote the libretto to *Così fan tutte* with a specific Viennese
audience in mind, whose theatrical preferences and experiences were
well known to him. But no matter how much he tried to accommodate this audience's expectations, it was inevitable that his text
would also betray his own Venetian background, in ways small and
large. (The presence of Albanian noblemen would have aroused far
less curiosity in that Adriatic port than in the Austrian capital, for
instance.) In view of the opera's central preoccupation with questions of fidelity and betrayal, it would seem worthwhile to turn to
the writings of that other notorious Venetian and libertine, Giacomo
Casanova, to see how they might resonate with the language and
subject matter of *Così*. Casanova is an particularly apt touchstone,
in that he was a friend of Da Ponte, an occasional visitor to Vienna
and its spectacles, and even tangentially involved with the shaping
of the text of *Don Giovanni*.[16]

Casanova's memoirs show him constantly under the spell of
fictions both literary and theatrical. Like Da Ponte, he had read
Orlando furioso 'a hundred times', 'knew it by heart' and made it a

guiding force in his life.[17] He was wont to refer to a situation he found himself in as a 'scène vraiment dramatique', or as a 'pièce [qui] touchait au dénouement' – not surprisingly, given that many of his friends and lovers came from theatrical circles. Indeed, the pages of his memoirs include numerous locutions that might easily have been taken from the libretto of *Così*. So sure is he, on one of the many occasions when he wagers on the virtue (or otherwise) of a woman, that he states his willingness to stake 'a hundred sequins, and a thousand, if you wish' (cf. I/1: *Alf.:* Cento zecchini. *Gugl.:* E mille, se volete).[18] Recounting an actress's protestations of outrage at his suggestion that her favours might be bought, he reverts to his native tongue and comments 'but I knew what really to think, for *così son tutte*'.[19] These and similar episodes in Casanova's memoirs (of which there are many), do much to remove the stain of 'inverisimilitude' from the plot of *Così*.

More importantly, in his memoirs Casanova gives voice to several of the same ideas on love as do the characters in *Così fan tutte*. He is more inclined to Despina's point of view than Alfonso's, despite the efforts of his father-figure, the very Alfonso-like 'Monsieur' (Matteo Giovanni) Bragadin. At one point the Venetian senator arranges a lesson by which he hopes to cure the young Casanova of gambling, but his pupil calls the demonstration 'too empirical', adding that 'I so feared his remedies that I preferred being sick to getting well by making use of them.'[20] In discussing his amorous affairs, Casanova is prone to the same worldly cynicism one finds in the speeches of Despina and in Pezzl's *Skizze*. A prudent husband will not wish to ask his wife if she is a virgin, he says, for he can never be sure of the truth.[21] Far from condemning two Parisian noblemen who trade wives, Casanova explains the arrangement 'according to the laws of gravitation'.[22] And in one of his frequent displays of casuistry, he justifies his infidelity to a current *innamorata* by noting that she is shut up in a convent and will never find out.[23] One of Casanova's more prolonged bursts of philosophizing concerns precisely the same issue as Alfonso's bet:

If, when I hear certain women call perfidious the men whom they accuse of inconstancy, I would have heard them assert that these men were planning to deceive them when they made a promise of eternal fidelity, I would say that they were right, and I would gladly join my complaints to theirs; but none of them can, since in general, at the instant when one falls in love, one only promises that which the heart dictates, and consequently their lamentations only excite in me the need to laugh. Alas! we love without consulting reason, and cease to love without its becoming any more involved than before.[24]

All but the last sentence of this speech might easily be put in the mouth of Don Alfonso. But whereas Casanova merely laments the irrationality of desire, Alfonso – and by the end of the opera, all the characters – realize that one may lessen the ill effects of this irrationality by ceasing to cherish illusions, and by trusting in societal bonds to provide the stability that is not to be expected from human affections alone.

Libertine philosophy is espoused with similar frankness in Choderlos de Laclos' *Les Liaisons dangereuses* (1782), whose protagonists coolly manipulate the affections of others in a manner suggestive of Da Ponte's Alfonso and Despina. Here, too, the game backfires, but the sufferings of the Marquise de Merteuil – constituting a sort of divine punishment for her sins – are of a very different order from those of Fiordiligi. And at the close of the novel's final letter, Mme de Volanges's declaration that reason is 'unable in the first place to prevent our misfortunes, [and] is even less equal to consoling us for them',[25] offers a moral diametrically opposed to that of *Così*.

Parties carrées

Not only the supposed immorality of *Così fan tutte*, but also the exaggerated symmetry of its plot has prevented many persons from taking the opera seriously. Aleksandr Ulybyshev, in his 1843 biography of Mozart, wrote that

The foursome [partie quarrée] joins up, advances, mixes, and unjoins with such regularity and symmetry, that the *ad hoc* scenes resemble rather well the figures of a contredanse.[26]

Ulybyshev's use of the expression 'partie carrée' was not neutral, for already in the eighteenth century this term for an outing by two couples had acquired licentious connotations – as one can sense from the ambiguous crossing of gazes in Watteau's painting of that title. Implicit in the biographer's criticism is the notion that the artifice and symmetry of Da Ponte's libretto precluded the serious exploration of psychological issues; Ulybyshev states explicitly that these features were incompatible with 'dramatic truth'. Much the same has been said of Goethe's novel *Die Wahlverwandtschaften* (Elective affinities) of 1809, in which predictions, coincidences and symmetries operate by a sort of human chemistry as two married couples meet, separate and realign, with disastrous results. In a manner reminiscent of *Così fan tutte*, the novel had a troubled reception throughout the nineteenth century, not fully coming into its own until recent decades. It is not even out of the question that Da Ponte and Mozart's opera was in the back of Goethe's mind as he wrote his novel, as he had been responsible for the Weimar première of *Così* in 1797, and for keeping it in the repertory long afterward. If so, then the novel is at least indirect evidence that Goethe appreciated full well the profundity of sentiment that lay beneath the opera's frivolous exterior.

Throughout *Die Wahlverwandtschaften* Goethe's narrative devices loudly call attention to themselves (as do Da Ponte's in *Così*), putting the issue of infidelity before the reader, and even in the mouths of the protagonists, well in advance of any actual betrayals. In the opening pages the principal couple, Eduard (originally named Otto) and Charlotte, discuss the number of persons the new moss hut in their garden might comfortably accommodate – four, they decide, in a self-conscious way that makes portentous the introduction of a second couple (the Captain and Ottilie) immediately afterward. In both opera and novel the names of the characters are endowed with almost talismanic significance: in their origins in Ariosto, in the one case, in their basis in the same (symmetrical) name Otto in the other.[27] There is even something of an Alfonso-figure in *Die Wahlverwandtschaften*, a wise old friend named Mittler ('mediator'), who acts as a catalyst at several points in the story. As in many a demonstration comedy, the title word 'Wahlverwandtschaften' is conspicuously introduced into the discussion. Responding to the Captain's use of the word to describe the spontaneous realignment of elements in a chemical reaction, Charlotte unwittingly predicts her own future affair with him, in so doing echoing Despina's talk of an amorous 'legge di natura' and Alfonso's of a 'necessità del core':

. . .here I would see not a choice, but rather a necessity of nature, and hardly even this: for in the end it is perhaps simply a matter of opportunity. Opportunity makes relationships, as it does thieves; and if one is speaking of natural bodies, then it seems to me that the choice lies solely in the hands of the chemist who brings them together. Once they are together, then God help them![28]

And as in Pezzl's *Skizze*, the theatre's falsely optimistic picture of life is attacked as dangerously misleading:

In the theatre we see a marriage as the final goal of a wish delayed by various obstacles through several acts, and in the moment that it is attained, the curtain falls, and the momentary satisfaction echoes on in us. In the world it is otherwise; there one goes on playing out of view, and when the curtain goes up again, one would not want to see or hear any of it.[29]

Beaumarchais, in his Revolutionary-era play *La Mère coupable*, had once again raised the curtain on the characters of *Le Barbier de Séville* and *Le Mariage de Figaro*, and revealed a number of dark consequences of their earlier actions. One might equally well ask how the lovers of *Così fan tutte* would fare, if examined in the same way.

The speech of the stonemason – a peripheral character – is perhaps the passage most laden with significance in all of Goethe's novel. As he lays the cornerstone for the new forest cottage, a project principally of the two characters drifting into adultery, the mason draws an analogy between the mortar he applies with his trowel, and the bonds of matrimony:

We could lay this cornerstone. . .without further ado, for it rests firmly by its own weight. But even here lime and mortar should not be lacking, for just as people who are naturally inclined towards one another are bound together even better when cemented by the law, thus also stones whose shapes already match are united even better by this binding power. . .[30]

The moral is lost on the protagonists, whose unhappy fates ultimately stand as an object lesson to the reader. The novel ends with a final, ironic symmetry, as Charlotte decides that the vault in which her husband and his lover Ottilie are buried will not hold any further remains – a reflection of the scene in the *Mooshütte* at the very beginning of the story, where she had similarly calculated the capacity of a small space. The artifice used here is very much like that employed throughout *Così fan tutte*, but in a context of sentimentality quite foreign to Da Ponte's æsthetic.

With much the same advocacy of reason and order (though with hardly a trace of humour), in *Die Wahlverwandtschaften* Goethe navigated the same shoals of trust and desire as had Da Ponte and Mozart in *Così fan tutte*. The formalism exhibited by this novel demonstrates the lingering appeal of Enlightenment ideals for at least some who had come to maturity during the Age of Reason. One senses this also in a much humbler literary work of the early nineteenth century, a dialogue in the *Theatralischer Guckkasten* (Theatrical peep-show) of 1807, by the Viennese actor, playwright and feuilletonist Joachim Perinet. Though he himself wrote exclusively for the city's German theatres, starting in the year of Mozart's death, Perinet expresses nostalgia for the golden age of Vienna's foreign stages, using as mouthpieces 'The Man' and 'Clown' ('Bajazzo', from the Italian *pagliaccio*):

Der Mann: Jetzt sehen Sie hier Glucks Alcest' und Iphigenie
              Mozart in seiner Blüthe, das Hauptgenie.
              Seinen Don Juan, Cosi fan tutti [sic] und Figaro,
Bajazzo: Ach! ich wollte die Zeiten wären noch so. . .

(*The Man:* Now you see here Gluck's *Alceste* and *Iphigénie*,
Mozart in his prime, the chief genius. His *Don Giovanni, Così fan
tutte* and *Figaro*, / *Clown:* Ah! I wish the times were still like
that. . .)[31]

As the Josephinian era receded ever farther into the past, the general
public found it increasingly difficult to relate to the rigorous symmetry, lighthearted philosophizing and general farcicality of *Così fan
tutte*. Productions of the opera consequently became less frequent,
and more prone to distortion. Yet Mozart had so well transmuted
into musical terms Da Ponte's fundamental sympathy for human
frailty, that open-minded listeners did not fail to be captivated by
the work. In more recent times, better acquaintance with the poetic
and musical conventions of Mozart's time, and with the rest of his
operas, has allowed one to see more specifically *how* Mozart and Da
Ponte achieved what they did. But as Bajazzo sensed, the times in
which such a work as *Così* might be created are long past.

6 The musical dramaturgy of the opera

Overall structure

As was seen in Chapter 4, Da Ponte's substitution of 'femmine' for 'amanti' in the Metastasian phoenix-quatrain skewed the symmetry of the accusation. Though Despina, echoing Ariosto's Rinaldo (43:49), tells her mistresses that the men, too, would find solace in other arms if given the chance, there is no demonstration of male inconstancy equivalent to the test the women are put through. One may attribute this to the poet's misogyny, or to his wish to avoid the repetitions that had marred Casti's *Grotta di Trofonio*, but in any case the decision had crucial repercussions for the structure and working-out of *Così*. Alfonso's contention that all women – 'gio-vani, vecchie, e belle, e brutte' – are potentially faithless, inspired Mozart to find musical analogues for the lovers' similarities, and for their differences. This did not escape the notice of Constanze Mozart. When asked her opinion of *Così fan tutte* by Vincent Novello in 1829, she

remarked that in 'Di scrivermi' (which I [Novello] guessed was one of his great favourites) you could actually fancy the sobs and tears of the per-formers – [she] also noticed the extraordinary *difference* of the melodies he has assigned to the various characters and the wonderful appropriateness of them.[1]

Given Da Ponte's intention to show that seductions attempted on women of differing characters would have the same result, his distri-bution of pieces in the opera is a logical one (see Table 6.1).

The singers' traditional rights to a certain number of sufficiently varied arias (here, one in each act) were respected,[2] but even so, the predominance of ensembles is striking. Furthermore, within each act, the arias for the four lovers come quite late; it is as if the creators were determined to deny the protagonists the usual operatic opportunities for reflection until after they have become ensnared in

95

Table 6.1: *Distribution of piece-types*

Act I

arias		(5),			11, 12,	14, 15,	17
duets		4,	7				
ensembles	1, 2, 3,		6,	9, 10,	13,	16	
choruses			8, (9)				
finale							18

Act II

arias	19,			24, 25, 26, 27, 28,	30	
duets		20, 21, (22), 23,			29	
ensembles		(22),				(30)
choruses		(21)				
finale						31

(The table is to be read chronologically, left to right; numbers are those of set pieces in the opera. Vertically aligned numbers represent pieces which can be classified under more than one type.)

the work's treacherous theatricality and musical beauties. The three consecutive trios for the men establish a strong male perspective at the outset, counterbalanced by the two pieces for the women which open Act II. The placement and distribution of duets is also worth noting. The two in the first act are for singers of the same sex, as are Nos. 20 and 21 (the latter *con coro*) in the second. Until the seduction duets of Act II, the original pairs of lovers interact only in the safety of larger ensembles, or in chaperoned recitatives. Dorabella's duet with Guglielmo comes before the series of five solo arias, and Fiordiligi's with Ferrando only afterward – this in order to contrast the unreflective capitulation of the one with the anguished, gradual submission of the other. The closest Despina and Alfonso come to singing a duet is in the highly irregular 'Quartetto', No. 22 (see below).[3]

In a general way, the distribution of pieces in an eighteenth-century opera was determined by the practical need to alternate long and short stage settings.[4] Arias tended to be sung within or near the proscenium arch, with the rear pairs of flats hidden by a backdrop, while most large ensembles and finales were performed using the entire length of the stage. The departure-pieces in *Così* (Nos. 5–10) naturally unfold at the shore; the gradual receding of the boat into the distance, commented upon in the recitative, makes obligatory the use of the full theatrical space. Unusually, the finale-like sextet in the first act (No. 13) takes place in a 'genteel room' (presumably a short stage-set), but this tableau is otherwise dominated by arias.

Versification

The librettist's delineation of character was likewise partly dependent on the poetic metres chosen for the set pieces.[5] Poets favoured shorter lines for the *parti buffe* and for scenes of action (on account of their close rhymes and incisive rhythms), and longer ones for more serious characters or situations. *Ottonario* (eight-syllable verse) was a librettist's workhorse, being susceptible of a variety of accentual patterns. Da Ponte uses this form for nearly ninety lines in the second finale (amounting to some 300 bars of music), before changing to *quinario* (five-syllable lines) in order to convey the panic caused by news of the soldiers' return. Note though in Example 6.1 how much rhythmic variety Mozart manages to introduce in Alfonso's exclamations, encouraged by the *sdrucciolo* (dactylic) ending of 'orribile'.

Example 6.1

Da Ponte's next change is to *decasillabo*, as a sign of the newly returned Ferrando and Guglielmo's composure – despite a quick costume change! The anapests characteristic of this verse-type were frequently lengthened at the beginning of a line, producing a stately gavotte rhythm (see Example 6.11b below). *Quinario* is used for the principal sections of both of Despina's arias, and for her appearance as the doctor in the first finale; the metre is as much a part of her personality as is her libertine philosophy. For the lines from 'Di pasta simile' onward in No. 12 Da Ponte alternates *piano* (normal, long-short) and *sdrucciolo* (dactylic, long-short-short) endings, with comic effect – as he does, more or less regularly, starting at the words 'Eccovi il medico' (bar 292 ff.) in the first finale. His use of this same verse-form in Dorabella's 'Smanie implacabili', which immediately precedes Despina's aria, can be no accident (see Examples 6.2a–b below).

The frequency with which the text of *Così fan tutte* calls attention to its status as poetry is one of the defining features of the opera. Not only are there passages in antique metres such as *terza* and *ottava rima*, and sudden concentrations of rhymes or of *sdrucciolo* endings in recitative (as in I/13); the verses themselves become the subject of discourse, in the suitors' burlesque, collaborative assault on the women's senses:

Gugl.:	Vista appena la luce	No sooner had we seen the light
	Di vostre fulgidissime pupille...	of your resplendent pupils...
Fer.:	...Che alle vive faville...	...than, to those lively sparks...
Gugl.:	...Farfallette amorose	...like amorous, suffering moths...
	agonizzanti...	
Fer.:	...Vi voliamo davanti...	...we came flying before you...
Gugl.:	...Ed ai lati ed a retro...	...and beside and behind you...
Fer.,}	...Per implorar pietade	...to implore your pity in plaintive
Gugl.:}	in flebil metro!	metres.

Example 6.2a

Example 6.2b

Tonal planning

On receiving Da Ponte's libretto for *Così fan tutte*, Mozart would have noted the nature and location of lyric numbers, and then made preliminary decisions on the keys in which to set them. We know that this was Salieri's practice, learnt from his mentor Gassmann,[6] and Mozart's letters on the genesis of *Die Entführung* suggest that he did no differently. Once *Così*'s keynote of C major was decided upon (and with it the key of No. 30), the next tonal choice was likely the key of the central finale. Only in *Idomeneo*, among Mozart's mature operas, does any but the last act end in the opera's tonic, and the composer returns sparingly to the keynote in the set pieces. His recourse to C major in the sextet of *Così* might be explained in terms of the noise called for at the end of its text, which an eighteenth-century orchestra could deliver most efficiently in this key. Similar reasoning might have come into play in the choice of D major, another trumpet-key, for the first finale. But it is tempting to see the neighbour-note relationship between beginning, middle and end as a large-scale reflection of the *Così*-trill which so dominates the overture.

In light of the conscious conventionality of many of Da Ponte's texts in *Così*, Mozart's tonal decisions were often fairly self-evident. A major suggested itself strongly for moments of amorous expression such as the first duet and Ferrando's 'Un'aura amorosa'. The military key of D was no less obvious in the case of 'Bella vita militar' (as an alternative to the keynote, C), and Mozart's decision to set Guglielmo's rondo 'Donne mie, la fate a tanti' in G major allowed C-trumpets and timpani to emerge in full splendour in the piece's military episode in the subdominant. Elsewhere in the work, the content of a given text pointed towards a range of possible keys, if not a single one. Mozart set the frankly comic pieces involving Despina and Guglielmo in F and G, keys with rustic associations. And for the opera's two apostrophes to the breezes, Nos. 10 and 21, Mozart used the 'covered' keys of E and E♭ major, with similar wind groups of flutes, clarinets, bassoons and horns. Taken as a whole, *Così* displays a wider range of tonalities than are found in Mozart's earlier Da Pontean comedies – or in his contemporaries' comic operas. This is perhaps to be explained by the prominence of serious or parodistic numbers, which pushed Mozart towards the wider tonal orbit (including considerable use of minor) characteristic of the baroque.

The issue of whether tonal connections between numbers of a Mozart opera were consciously planned (or perceivable by the listener) has been much argued.[7] Certainly they were, in cases where numbers or sections were contiguous. But such places are relatively infrequent in *Così*, apart from the two finales, and the laughing trio which issues directly from No. 15. The most obvious juxtaposition is actually a break between scenes: the nearly instantaneous changes of sets in eighteenth-century theatres allowed audiences to hear with full effect the contrast of the trumpet-and-drums C major of No. 3 with the softer-hued A major of the second scene's duet. The first appearance of 'Bella vita militar' is similarly flanked by pieces a third away (with brief recitatives in between), thus highlighting the jarring effect of the signal for departure. Otherwise, the pieces in *Così* are separated by recitatives of considerable length – even the opening three trios, whose keys (as numerous commentators have noted) spell out the opera's tonic triad. Yet it was not impossible for spectators to perceive certain tonal returns, if these were accompanied by details of instrumentation, harmony and motif from a key's earlier appearance. There is certainly no mistaking the return of C major in the central section of the second seduction duet. Not only was it a reprise of music heard in No. 3, 'Una bella serenata', the piece's harmonic plan also recalled that of the A-major trio 'Ah taci, ingiusto core' in *Don Giovanni*, in which a C-major serenade – itself a quotation – emerges unexpectedly from the key of E (major, in that case).

In a work as dependent on parody as *Così*, characteristic details of harmony tend to be connected with the operatic conventions adopted or mocked by Mozart. A number of these will emerge in the discussion below, but in general one might mention the characters' propensity towards cadential evasions. The overture points the way with the deceptive cadence of the motto, but the deceptive cadences in the opera proper tend more towards hysteria than this one. In the opening number, the officers' *forte* syncopations in their repeated cadential phrase 'che torto le fa' suggest that they protest rather too much at Alfonso's allegations regarding their women's virtue. Soon afterwards, Alfonso piles exclamation upon exclamation at the end of his woeful greeting of the ladies in No. 5, taking advantage of the exclamatory-sounding verb 'ho' (have). And in the following piece the entire ensemble similarly bewails the men's impending departure; note how the singers outdo each other from one melisma to the next, as if in a competition of grief (see Example 6.3).

Example 6.3

Deceptive cadences are at their most prominent at precisely the
moment when Ferrando is being undeceived. As Guglielmo shows
him the portrait that Dorabella has given away, he breaks into an
accompanied recitative which pushes to extremes both the textual
and musical clichés of opera seria. Ferrando's seemingly final
cadences are twice frustrated, and indeed the aria which follows is
for Guglielmo, not him (see Example 6.4).

In the same spirit as these deceptive moves are the many fermatas
which mark points of arrival. These the singers were free to exag-
gerate; Mozart sometimes required them to do so, with written-out
ornamentation (see Example 6.6 below).

Amidst all this exaggeration, one still finds many examples of the
naturalness which Mozart brought to all his comic operas. Nos. 3, 5,
12, 13 and 26 all begin on the dominant – in two cases so as to
afford the singer time to reflect before responding to a question or a
request.[8] And lest one think that deception and parody need always
go hand-in-hand, in the Terzettino, No. 10, there is the most
sublime of all deceptive cadences, on the word 'desir', to remind us
that there can be beauty as well as peril in self-delusion (see
Example 6.5).

The magic of this moment is brought about by the confluence of
several factors: the substitution of a diminished-seventh chord, over
a dominant pedal, for the expected tonic; the coming-together of the
voices after a passage in invertible counterpoint; and the first use in
the piece of both horns and flutes. On a second attempt at the cadence the spacing of the diminished chord is rearranged, and the
flutes help carry Fiordiligi's line past the upper tonic to a sustained

Example 6.4

Example 6.5

g#", the highest pitch thus far. One can only hope that Alfonso's much-vaunted 'reason' has something with which to compensate the lovers for illusions as wondrous as this.

'Io crepo se non rido': tears and laughter in the 'farewell' quintet

With *Così fan tutte* Da Ponte and Mozart succeeded in creating a drama at once amusing and profound, out of subject matter that was, at least potentially, oppressively terrifying. That Mozart had experienced (or suspected) sexual betrayal in his own relations with the sisters Weber no doubt contributed to the keenness of his insights into his opera's characters – insights audible as much in the radiance of the music with which they seduce or are seduced, as in their outpourings of anguish. Perhaps because so much of the drama in *Così* centres on the gradual awakenings of suspicion or desire, and because the male protagonists are disguised in all but the opening and closing scenes, the piece seems often to exhibit a less than straightforward relationship between music and text. In his 1843 biography of the composer, Aleksandr Ulybyshev voiced the by then ritual scorn for Da Ponte's libretto, and proceeded to articulate with unusual clarity the 'quandary' that he and many others supposed Mozart to have faced.

It is clear that if Mozart had wanted to fill in this canvas with the respect he normally accorded the work or his poets, if he had looked, above all, for dramatic truth in a drama where everything is completely false, one of two things would have happened. Mozart would have recognized the poem to be uncomposable and would have abandoned it; or, he would have had to create bad music, a score without wit and without soul, which would have been another impossibility for him. Trapped in this double impasse of a dilemma, our hero of necessity did what Italian composers do out of habit or by design. He treated the text lightly and seemed at times to forget it entirely.

The disparity between words and music was not as wide as in most operas of Rossini, Ulybyshev says:

No, the text of *Così fan tutte* is never a parody of this sort. True, the music does not always match the spirit of the situations and the feelings of the characters, such as the librettist conceived them; but it never actually contradicts them; it only gives them a different interpretation, much more delicate, more varied, more dramatic and more lyrical, but equally and fully compatible with the givens of the subject.[9]

Even though Ulybyshev is perhaps unfair in assuming that an opera's text may be considered apart from its (potential) musical setting, he has identified a genuine issue with regard to *Così*, for at numerous points in the opera there is an undeniable ambiguity as to where the boundary lies between pathos and parody. The issue is specifically raised in the text at several points, in Da Ponte's opposition of 'piangere' and 'ridere'. To determine whether or how Mozart reinterpreted, exaggerated or shaded the meanings of his text, one must first understand the conventions within which he was working. But even taking these into account, we have to consider that at least some of the score's ambiguities are intentional, part of a strategy by which the spectator is made to experience the same uncertainties as do the characters on stage.

A modern audience's experience of *Così fan tutte* is necessarily coloured by the knowledge that, at the time of the première, its composer had but a short time to live. Noting thematic parallels to *Die Zauberflöte*, another work of enlightenment through trial, Stefan Kunze called *Così* 'a work of farewell' from illusion, and from former ways of life and love.[10] The aura of wistfulness that hangs over *Così* is enhanced by our recognition of melodies and harmonies from elsewhere in the composer's *Spätwerk* – most notably, the exalted cadence of the embarkation quintet (No. 9), which Mozart reused a year later in his setting of the motet 'Ave, verum corpus',

K618. Such associations have led many listeners to perceive this and other 'late-sounding' pieces in the opera as completely serious. In Fiordiligi's *rondò*, for instance, Kunze found 'no trace of irony or even parody'; '[o]therwise Beethoven could scarcely have taken it as a model for Leonore's aria in *Fidelio*. . .'.[11] But in fact, the simultaneous portrayal of opposed emotions was a well-established concept in eighteenth-century æsthetics, one especially praised in the critical writings of Diderot. In painting, this technique enabled the viewer to extrapolate beyond the temporal frame of the image; on the stage, a skilled actor could differentiate between those attitudes shown to the other characters, and those revealed to the audience. The unsettling conjunction in *Così fan tutte* of comic texts and sublime music must not be explained away; their coexistence is an acknowledgement of the opera's theatricality – of the fact that very real emotions are being stimulated through artificial means.

The workings of such a strategy can be seen in the above-cited quintet, No. 9, which is sandwiched between repetitions of the march 'Bella vita militar'.[12] The couples' parting endearments are ostensibly serious, but are treated in burlesque fashion by poet and composer alike. Fiordiligi entreats Guglielmo to write her each day; Dorabella requests *two* daily missives from her lover. The stage directions specify that the sisters are weeping, as is clear also from the typography of the original libretto:

Fior.:	Di...scri...ver...mi...	Swear to write me every day,
	ogni...gior...no	
	Giurami...vita...mia (*piangendo*)	my life (*weeping*).
Dor.:	Due vol...te...an...cora...	Write me two times a day, even,
	Tu...scri...vimi...se...puoi...	if you can.
Ferr.:	Sii certa, o cara...	Be assured, my dear...
Gugl.:	Non...dubitar mio bene...	Do not doubt it, my beloved...

Mozart comically elides isolated syllables from adjacent words ('Di scri- ver- *mi o*- gni gior- no', 'Due vol- *te an*- co- ra'), and accompanies the women's broken declamation with repeated-note sobs in the violins. Fiordiligi demonstrates constancy by clinging to the fifth scale degree for six full bars, in octaves with the bassoons; she and they move away from their C's precisely at the point where she sings the word 'costante'! Just before the line 'Mi si divide il cor, bell'idol mio', the violas, in unison up to now, 'divide' into two parts. To all of this Alfonso can only mutter to himself 'Io crepo se non rido!' (I'll burst if I don't laugh!).

Each of the musical details just enumerated seconds the humour of the text – as Constanze Mozart seems to have perceived. These features likewise mark the quintet as belonging to a family of similar *entrecoupé* pieces in opera buffa, which could be either mock-tragic (as in Alfonso's No. 5) or truly serious. And yet, what the listener notices most in No. 9 is its luminous texture and harmonies, which coexist with the comic elements without in any way interfering with them. Mozart fills out the vocal texture one part at a time, over the pizzicato basses' six-fold cadential pattern which seems to hold off indefinitely the moment of departure.[13] At bar 7 the lovers leave off their fragmentary utterances and soar in new harmonic directions; at the same time the viola line is freed from its previous oscillation, and moves in gentle counterpoint with the voices, as a wordless, sympathetic observer. As the women respond to the men's farewell, a crescendo, the splitting of the viola line and a deceptive cadence combine to suggest a sudden welling-up of emotion. And as the four lovers sing together for the first time in the piece, the clarinets, unheard until now, enter with the bassoons and double the voice parts in their cadence, whose repetition is sensuously ornamented by Fiordiligi. Comedy returns surreptitiously under the final 'addio's with Alfonso's tonic-dominant ostinato, after which a single orchestral chord wrenches the lovers and the audience back to the cheerful irony of 'Bella vita militar'.

A simultaneously comic and poignant ensemble is perhaps untypical of run-of-the-mill opere buffe, in which uncomplicated affects tend to be presented quite directly, but Da Ponte's revered Metastasio teaches one to expect such a flood of conflicting emotions in scene of a leave-taking. The example below comes from *Demetrio*, the opera which supplied Da Ponte with the phoenix-quatrain of the second terzetto in *Così*:

Non so frenare il pianto,	I cannot curb the tear that falls
Cara, nel dirti addio:	While on my tongue the farewell dies;
Ma questo pianto mio	Yet 'tis not grief alone that calls
Tutto non è dolor.	These trickling waters from my eyes.
È meraviglia, è amore,	Repentance, wonder, hope, and love,
È pentimento, è speme,	Th' emotion, which I feel, impart:
Son mille affetti insieme	At once a thousand thoughts I prove,
Tutti raccolti al cor.	That crowd tumultuous to my heart.[14]

(Metastasio, *Demetrio*, II/12)

It is unclear to what extent Da Ponte encouraged the lyric effusions in the quintet. The piece's text consists of the *versi sciolti – settenari* and *endecasillabi* (7- and 11-syllable lines) – normally used for recitative, and indeed, Mozart called the piece a 'Recitativo'. But a rhymed couplet in the preceding simple recitative ('stanno'/'affanno'), sung in comic fashion by the men and the women in pairs, is possibly a signal that a concerted piece was to follow. The overtly comic content of No. 9 ends with the unorthodox punctuation, from which point all the lines are rhymed, as normally in lyric numbers. Two other *endecasillabo* texts in *Così* – Alfonso's (unnumbered) Sannazaro quotation, and the *ottava* of No. 30 – were orchestrated and set in arioso style, which suggests that Da Ponte expected a similar treatment here.

Symmetry and difference: two duets

The musical parallelisms in *Così* are at their most obvious in the duet 'Ah guarda, sorella', which begins the demonstration that 'all women are like that'. The clarinets' and bassoons' dulcet melody in thirds, the airy string accompaniment, and A-major tonality announce the setting by the shore, and offer the opera's first sounds (as opposed to talk) of love. The ritornello mainly previews Fiordiligi's music: her sighs as she contemplates her fiancé's portrait, and her melismatic cadence which illustrates the word 'ritrovar' by 'finding' the tonic on its final syllable (see Example 6.6).

Such literal illustrations are by no means uncommon in Mozart; the composer himself points out several in a letter describing Belmonte's second aria in *Die Entführung aus dem Serail*.[15] Whereas Fiordiligi emphasizes the 'fair mouth' and 'noble mien' of her lover Guglielmo, Dorabella adopts a more declamatory style and lets the staccato string accompaniment of bars 35–42 describe the fire and arrows shot off by Ferrando's glances. Having contrasted their lovers (or rather, their tastes in lovers), in the transitional section which follows (bars 50–65) the sisters show signs of envy, and incorporate elements from each other's descriptions. Exchange is also evident in the final bars of transition before the Allegro, as the sisters sing of their happiness in mirror image:[16]

> Fior.:   Felice son io!
> Dor.:   Io sono felice!

In the faster second section of the duet (still in *senario*), the two sisters, singing together for the first time, make a vow to Cupid that is a pendant to the wager their menfolk have made:

Example 6.6

Example 6.7

Se questo mio core
Mai cangia desio,
Amore mi faccia
Vivendo penar.

(If this heart ever changes desire, let Cupid make me suffer a
life of torture.)

Mention of Cupid brings a drastic slowing of declamation for a
burlesque invocation of the god: the sisters respond to the rocketing
cellos and bassoons with exquisitely ornamentated fermatas, the
second of them Adagio. The rising and then falling chromaticism of
the cadence phrases imparts an erotic ambiguity to the significance
of 'penar' (see Example 6.7).

The long coda consists mainly of self-inflicted vocal tortures:
demonstrating constancy, Dorabella holds the '-nar' of 'penar' on an
e" for nine full bars, while Fiordiligi declaims the entire quatrain to
falling and rising arpeggios. But the idea of steadfastness is under-
mined when the singers exchange material; the repeat of the passage
is in a higher register, with Fiordiligi sustaining an even more painful
a". The comic *forte* outbursts in their cadential perorations herald
many more in their music to come.

The suggestions of exchange in the sisters' duet about constancy
are followed by others in the soldiers' duettino 'Al fato dan legge',
No. 7. The piece is often omitted in performance, on account of its
rather meagre melodic inspiration, but its several pointed references
to No. 4 give the duettino an importance beyond its modest scope.
The pieces are alike in poetic metre and instrumentation; in the
men's duet, too, the god of Love is invoked, and rising and falling
chromatic lines are neatly balanced. And once again there is a
cadential pun: melismas on the word 'tornar' (set against sustained
notes) which refuse to 'return' to the tonic degree. As in the coda to
No. 4, the singers exchange their material (see Example 6.8).

The game of finding the tonic is connected to more general prob-
lems in the melodic design of the piece. Each of Ferrando's short
phrases gains but one pitch over the last, until the line stalls on the
fourth scale degree – reflecting the intentionally comic mismatch
between the short *senario* verses and the overly elaborate thoughts
the men try to express with them (see Example 6.9).

It is tempting to see this melody's tentative launching as an
analogue of the soldiers' reluctant 'departure', and the subsequent
exchange of material on 'tornar' as representing their switch of
partners on returning.

There are further examples in *Così* of such local symmetries. In
the larger ensembles (Nos. 6, 13) and the finale of Act I, for

Example 6.8

Example 6.9

instance, the men's and women's voices (respectively) remain parallel with studied artificiality. The initial vocal phrases of No. 20, the duet wherein the sisters choose their new gallants, simultaneously equate and differentiate, through distinctive rhythmic details superimposed on similar melodic profiles and harmonies. And near the end of the opera, there is melodic symmetry of motion upward and downward by fourths as Alfonso explains that the lesson of the charade is in a sense symmetrical after all (see Example 6.10).

Prediction, recollection and oblivion.

As in many a 'demonstration comedy', the very title of *Così fan tutte* foretells the outcome of the drama. The critic Friedrich Rochlitz was much impressed with the way the composer seconded his librettist in this connection:

Example 6.10

He has the motto recited there [in No. 30] in the manner of a chorale, and also towards the start of the Overture, after a few imposing bars, which invite the listener to expect something highly significant, sure enough, the melody of that signature of the whole is as plainly stated as if it were piped from a tower. Can one mistake this? Could one do it any more neatly?[17]

An array of predictions and reminiscences pervades *Così fan tutte*, interlocking like gears in a well-made machine. Da Ponte draws our attention to this aspect of the piece, with Despina's self-serving comment just before the first finale:

> Quando Despina macchina una cosa,
> Non può mancar d'effetto.
>
> (When Despina plots a thing, it cannot fail).

Mozart seized upon only a portion of the textual echoes Da Ponte had planted in the libretto. Conversely, there are musical reminiscences which function independently of any overt textual links, serving to communicate ironies across long spans of time, or underscore affinities between characters.

Obviously connected with the opera's motto is the trial of fidelity which demonstrates it. We know that the lesson has been learnt when, in the penultimate section of the second finale, the officers renounce any further proofs ('. . .ma la prova io far non vo"). But curiously, when in the opening number of the opera Alfonso advises them of the foolishness of such an inquiry ('Tai prove lasciamo. . .'), the philosopher's words are largely hidden in the musical texture. This is nevertheless dramatically realistic: the intercutting and over-lapping of lines show how, in their anger, the officers have ceased to listen to their friend. Mozart transforms the sweeping scales here (bars 36–7) which illustrate the soldiers' unsheathing of their swords into a violin motif in semiquavers, whose aimless motion is a good analogue for the 'foolish desire' of which Alfonso warns. Despina is accompanied by a very similar motif in the Sestetto, No. 13 (bars 22–5), as she contemplates the bizarre-looking suitors; when the voices join shortly thereafter, she sings the same motif in augmentation.

Only slightly less wide is the frame of references to drinking, in the 'brindis replicati' (repeated toasts) proposed in No. 3 and the canonic toast of the second finale (see Example 6.16b below). (In the first finale, the drink is no *brindisi*, but rather a draught of arsenic!) Fiordiligi leads the toast at the wedding banquet, urging her com-panions to erase all memory of the rancour that has preceded. This is too much for Guglielmo, the lover whom she has betrayed just two numbers previously – though his refusal to join the quartet has also been explained in terms of the problem his bass voice posed for Mozart's invertible counterpoint. Fiordiligi's suggestion is ironic,

Example 6.11a

Example 6.11b

since in her *rondò* she had sung of driving away all memory of her illicit passion. (Whether by coincidence or design, the enharmonic shift with which Mozart rouses the new couples from their reverie at the end of the canon brings back the E major of the *rondò*.) The true author of the canon's text might well be said to be Despina, who in No. 22 had put the words 'Scordiamci del passato' (Let us forget the past) into the mouths of the still timid sisters.

Da Ponte planted many other seeds of irony in his libretto, not least in Fiordiligi and Dorabella's first duet, where he has them call upon Cupid to visit them with torments should they ever prove inconstant. At the start of the first finale the sisters declare their lives to be 'a sea of torments', though by the next act it is the suitors who complain of amorous pains, in their serenade (No. 21); these become 'sweet torment' by the end of the first love duet (No. 23). Upon discovering the marriage contract in the second finale (bars 434 ff.), the newly-returned soldiers threaten to spill their rivals' blood 'in torrents, in rivers, in seas' – bringing the theme full circle. The violins' comically exaggerated swordplay here is itself a recollection (of the soldiers' challenge to Alfonso in the opening number), as is also the rising sequence of bars 453–5, which was heard in the duet wherein the sisters had giddily anticipated a flirtation (see Examples 6.11a–b).[18]

Independently of his librettist, Mozart provided a pair of unmistakable references to cuckolding, at key entrances of the two soldiers. As we see them for the first time in their Albanian costumes, they implore Despina's aid in seducing her mistresses, in horn-harmonies which foretell that the pairing will be reversed; there is similar writing upon the officers' 'return' in the second finale, just as the talk turns to fidelity. This device had already been used fleetingly (though with emphasis supplied by a fermata) at the midpoint of No. 2, to contradict each lover's assertion that his fiancée is the phoenix cited by Alfonso. Purely musical reminiscences are especially concentrated in the approach to the dénouement, helping counteract the forgetfulness which so afflicts the four lovers in this opera. As if to fortify her resolve while resisting Ferrando's advances in the accompanied recitative before No. 24, Fiordiligi sings the phrase 'tu vuoi tormi la pace' (you wish to steal my peace of mind) to a melting harmonic progression (G minor to an E♭ chord in first inversion) she had used to the words 'l'intatta fede' in the preparation to her first aria. This is itself a near-quotation (*così fan tutte!*) of music Dorabella had sung before *her* first aria (No. 11), as she remonstrates with Despina for mocking her sorrow (see Examples 6.12a–c).

The origins of this progression – and the undulating string figure which accompanies it in two of its appearances – in Mozart's own *Idomeneo* (in the recitative preceding Ilia's first aria, bars 36–7) suggests that the composer wished to emphasize the seriousness with which the two heroines take their predicaments, even while under-

Example 6.12a

Example 6.12b

Example 6.12c

scoring their reliance on convention. (The wavering string figure closes both the Quintetto, No. 6 in *Così*, and the quartet in the earlier opera, which is likewise in Eb.)[19] A more immediate intermediary for Ex. 6.12c, with nearly identical writing for low strings, is found in the music accompanying Donna Anna's attempts to cool

Example 6.12d

the ardour of her fiancé in *Don Giovanni*, in the recitative before No. 23 ('Non mi dir, bell'idol mio'; see Example 6.12d).[20]

The *sang-froid* shown by Mozart in plundering music of such seriousness from his own compositional œuvre, for use in a comic opera, is worthy of the Diderot of the *Paradoxe sur le comédien*, and an indication of the complexity of tone of this opera generally.

More fleeting, and probably unconscious, is the resemblance between a melodic figure near the end of Ferrando's No. 24, another in Dorabella's final aria, and the theme of the finale of Mozart's last piano concerto (begun 1788 or 1789), all of which pieces share the key of B♭ (see Examples 6.13a–c).

This musical connection between members of a 'right' couple pales in importance when compared to the longer quotation within No. 29, as Ferrando is seducing Fiordiligi, of music he had sung in the third terzetto. This recall is particularly unsettling, as it is Fiordiligi who, though having never heard the terzetto, first slips into the C-major melody to which he had sung the words 'Una bella

Example 6.13a

Ferrando: Ah ces - sa - te, spe - ran - ze fal - la - ci!

Example 6.13b

Dorabella: Se nel tuo pet - to ei sie - de, s'e - gli ti bec - ca qui,

Example 6.13c

serenata / Far io voglio alla mia dea' – which referred not to her, but to Dorabella. (The A-major key signature continues unaltered for sixteen bars, as a sign of her resistance, changing only after the cadence in bar 39.) Details of texture as well as melody call the earlier passage to mind; the contrary motion (bars 29–30 in the duet) is even more apt than originally, as here Ferrando is (suggestively) unsheathing his sword. Only with the cluster of recalls beginning at bar 496 in the second finale does the quotation of earlier music fully break through to the consciousness of the singers. Ferrando's self-introduction was a compositional loose end, as we have seen, but Guglielmo's nearly literal reminders of the 'ritrattino' and of the role played by the 'magnetico Signor Dottore' allow the women to connect the quite different amorous worlds of before and after the departure of their fiancés. There was precedent for such a strategy: as the soubrette Vespina unmasks in the dénouement of Haydn's *L'infedeltà delusa* (1773, Coltellini/Friberth), she recalls music she had sung in two of the four disguises she had assumed during the opera.[21]

Opera seria models: convention and citation

Mozart's music for *Così fan tutte* does not merely make use of operatic conventions, it continually thrusts them into the foreground, imparting to the work a sense of theatricality more pronounced even than in *Le nozze di Figaro*. According to Rochlitz, Mozart delighted in improvising parodies of Italian composers and singers, although, with a single exception, he 'did not take the time to write out such things'.[22] Though ever-present, the parody of serious opera in *Così* is far from uniform in nature or purpose, and seldom approaches the outright caricature that Rochlitz says went into Mozart's improvisations. In most cases there is simply an accumulation of exaggerated verbal and musical details, which subtly undermine the characters' ostensible seriousness of purpose.[23]

As the instigator of the masquerade, Don Alfonso is also the opera's most adept manipulator of verbal and musical styles. He is the only character to quote directly from an opera seria, with his quatrain from Metastasio's *Demetrio*. But since (as Rochlitz notes) Alfonso cannot take anything seriously,[24] he sings this dictum *scherzando*, to a repetitious, insinuating line which marks it as a familiar but inconvenient truth. When Alfonso does have recourse to seria style, his text from Sannazaro ('Nel mare solca. . .') is several centuries too old. The music illustrates each of the images in the text, in successive four-bar segments whose style draws upon exact contemporaries of Metastasio. The officers and Despina also resort to parody, though as the action progresses, Ferrando especially seems less and less aware of whether he is feigning. In their attempt at seduction following No. 13 (quoted above), the strangely garbed Albanians adopt the extravagant language of seventeenth-century love poetry, which Mozart cloaks in appropriately antique-sounding string halos. The parody is not recognized as such initially: Dorabella's exclamation 'Numi, che sento?' (in best opera seria style), in reaction to the first chord, bodes well for the suitors. Late in the opera, when Ferrando interrupts Fiordiligi's preparations for a battlefield reunion with Guglielmo, he still sings in opera seria clichés ('. . .meschinello io mi morrò'), and in a minor mode that was quite outdated in late-eighteenth-century opera. But as he pushes the assault further, the boundary between sincerity and insincerity becomes tenuous indeed. Having gained the advantage over Fiordiligi, Ferrando slows to a Larghetto in triple meter, and implores her not to delay in surrendering. His melody, like that of

Example 6.14a

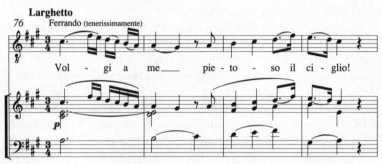

Example 6.14b

E nel___ tuo, nel mio___ bic - chie - ro

si_____ som - mer - ga o - gni___ pen - sie - ro

the Larghetto canon of the second finale, is accompanied by strings alone, and reaches to the upper tonic in its sixth bar, where Mozart exposes Ferrando's voice as an illustration of the word 'sol' (alone); see Examples 6.14a–b.

If Despina may be said to have dictated Fiordiligi's sentiments in the canon, Ferrando has taught her to sing in this manner. And yet there is a sly lasciviousness in his words – '. . .in me alone you will find a spouse, a lover, and more, if you desire' – which causes one to question whether he means them entirely in earnest.

The sisters' first-act arias present the work's most ambitious uses of the forms and language of opera seria. The humour of Dorabella's 'Smanie implacabili' derives almost entirely from its context, for the piece exhibits the same mythic vocabulary, broken declamation, harmonic language and instrumentation as Elettra's 'D'Oreste, d'Aiace' in *Idomeneo* – where such histrionics were actually called for.[25] The preceding recitative, as we have seen, already points to *Idomeneo* – though initially it gives the impression more of one of Mozart's improvised satires. Just prior to the aria, Dorabella orders Fiordiligi and Despina to leave her alone in her grief; yet all three

remain at the aria's end, the sisters hurling themselves gracelessly
into chairs. While Dorabella's gasping declamation and sighing
cadences tend towards excess, in construction her piece is not
significantly different from Elettra's: both are bi-partite sonata
forms, with only brief harmonic development as the text starts over.
Mozart's handling of the winds – traditionally used to invoke the
underworld – is even more varied and sophisticated in the later
parody aria. From bar 9 the flagellating string ostinato is supported
by the horns and then bassoons, who seem to embody the 'smanie'
addressed by Dorabella. Plangent clarinets accompany her half-
cadence, after which they and the bassoons (plus flutes, upon repetition) illustrate her pangs of anguish with mis-accented suspensions.
As Dorabella mentions the furies, flutes and bassoons in octaves
engage her in dialogue. On the climactic word 'orribile' Mozart
brings together all four pairs of winds for the first time in the piece,
and finally allows Dorabella to sustain her line, bending it through a
painful G♭ and successive diminished-seventh chords towards the
piece's median cadence. The 'horrible' choir then reenters to help
effect the modulation as the text begins anew. Mozart varies the
winds' deployment imaginatively in the reprise, adding groaning
sevenths in the bassoons just after the tonic is reestablished (bars
49–52). At 'orribile' the full winds again help Dorabella through her
G♭, to G♮ and then A♭, her highest pitch in the piece. The coda (bars
75 ff.) runs aground on a deceptive cadence on this same word and
pitch, whereupon Dorabella and the now unaccompanied winds
unfurl the diminished seventh to a resumption of the sighing
cadences that had ended the first half.

Though Fiordiligi claims to be unimpressed by the Albanians'
suit, the aria with which she responds, 'Come scoglio immoto resta',
is filled with ambiguities of which she seems quite unaware. The
piece has usually been seen as a parody of the Metastasian simile or
metaphor aria,[26] but the 'Come'/'Così' opposition of its first stanza
never actually occurs in that poet's works. Rather, this formula
seems to have originated in operas from the earlier generation of
Apostolo Zeno, and was widely imitated by librettists of works both
serious and comic. Thus in Goldoni's *Amore in caricatura* (1761) one
character sings a love aria whose quatrains begin with the words
'Siccome' and 'Così', and is answered sarcastically with another
'Come. . .' aria. The days of da capo arias being long past, Da
Ponte confines his metaphor to the first quatrain of Fiordiligi's aria
(quoted in Chapter 4), and provides two more stanzas, out of which
Mozart built an imposing three-tempo aria:

. . . .
Con noi nacque quella face
Che ci piace e ci consola;
E potrà la morte sola
Far che cangi affetto il cor.

Rispettate, anime ingrate,
Questo esempio di costanza;
E una barbara speranza
Non vi renda audaci ancor.

(In us is kindled that torch which delights and consoles, and
death alone can make our hearts change affections. Honour, ye
heartless souls, this example of constancy, and may no insolent
hope again render you bold.)

Fiordiligi's words are meant sincerely, as were those of Ariosto's
Bradamante which inspired them. Da Ponte undercuts Fiordiligi
slightly through his use of such a time-worn formula, but far more
damaging to her credibility is what Mozart does in his musical
setting. The beginning of her aria continues as if in accompanied
recitative (though with more clearly directed harmony), as Fiordiligi
exaggerates even further her leaps between registers, before landing
on a very premature climax in bar 13. Not only is her melody a
glaring contradiction of the immobility of which she sings, but her
(notated) repeated notes on the words 'scoglio' and 'resta' demand
to be sung as prosodic appoggiaturas, according to late-eighteenth-
century practice (see Example 6.15).

The resumption of Fiordiligi's melody with the 'così. . .' half of
the metaphor shows up as ludicrous the firm tonic cadence of the
initial dependent clause. This violation of musical syntax provokes
a wordless commentary, as the pizzicato bass of bars 23 ff. dupli-
cates, in the same key, Alfonso's line at 'Io crepo se non rido' in
No. 9, against a 'constant' pedal point in the violas such as
Fiordiligi and the bassoons had supplied there. In the approach to
the aria's median cadence further ridiculous leaps again illustrate the
change of heart Fiordiligi swears will never occur.

Following a ritornello whose decorated scales seem calculated to
incite the singer to move fretfully to and fro across the stage, the
opening text is reset as a transition to the Più Allegro. Mozart's
music in this final section is an invitation to the stage director, for
the repeated-note violin figure clearly represents the suitors'
advances, which Fiordiligi attempts to repel. They ignore her plea
for 'respect', jumping in on the end of her phrase, and then swarm

Example 6.15

around her in imitative triplets, like the 'Farfallette amorose agoniz-
zanti' of the recitative just previous (see Example 6.16).

The violins' triplets tempt Fiordiligi/Ferrarese into the triplet
coloratura at which she was so adept, after which she shows off her
low register – against violins *in altissimo* – in the first of two
cadential themes. But there are further indignities in store for her:
Mozart first denies her the expected tonic harmony under her final
high Bb, and then the suitors prevent her from exiting – a grave
affront, after a showpiece aria such as this.

As with Dorabella's No. 11, the humour in Ferrando's 'Un'aura
amorosa' lies mainly in its context: this illustration of a Petrarchan
conceit – that a lover needs no sustenance other than an amorous
breath from his beloved – is introduced by Guglielmo's abrupt comment about his empty stomach.[27] Mozart creates a slightly antique
feeling through his emphasis of second beats in the triple-metre
melody. Antique, too, are the string accompaniment, the final hemiola
cadence and the dotted beginning of the coda (reminiscent of Elvira's
'Ah fuggi il traditor'), which melts into an echo of the vocal climax.
For this number Mozart chooses an ABA form reminiscent of the
old da capo aria, though with a middle section that hints at sonata

Example 6.16

form, with its initial modulation and independent second idea at
bar 30.[28] The return (traditionally sung *pianissimo*) is magically
rescored, with afterbeats provided by the winds, which have been
absent since the opening flourish. The first bassoon's downward
chromatic inflection in bar 43 (a reflection of a gesture repeated four
times in the second half of the A melody) adds a touch of uncommon poignancy. The exalted vocal coda (incorporating elements from
the melody's middle section) and orchestral postlude mark Ferrando
as one of Mozart's noblest characters, even in his delusions.

Many commentators have described the serious arias in the
second act (Nos. 24, 25 and 27) as essentially untouched by irony.
Fiordiligi, more than any of the lovers, senses the gravity of entering
into an illicit liaison, which makes all the more tragic her helpless-
ness in avoiding it; Ferrando, through his music, reaches a higher
level of passion than is evident in his sublimated first aria. By virtue
of its form – a full-scale *rondò* in two tempos – Fiordiligi's 'Per
pietà, ben mio, perdona' commands attention as the most important
in the sequence of five arias in this act. Adriana Ferrarese would
have accepted nothing less, given the roles she had taken in her
career thus far (see Chapter 7). Knowing this, Da Ponte and Mozart
used the features peculiar to this aria-type in order to plant clues as
to her future actions.

Even if Fiordiligi herself is utterly sincere, Da Ponte gently mocks
her predicament by ending her preceding *recitativo accompagnato*
with a most Metastasian list of guilt-related affects; these Mozart
undercuts with a uniform accompaniment of tremolo strings, illustrating the 'ardour' to which she had just confessed. The opening
slow section of the aria exhibits the same extreme leaps between

registers as in 'Come scoglio'. But these are applied more appropriately than in la Ferrarese's earlier aria: low notes for the 'shame' (vergogna), and high for the 'horror' she feels on account of her attraction to the mysterious stranger. Da Ponte exploits the convention of bringing back text from the opening part of a *rondò* in the second, faster section, in that he has Fiordiligi sing of expunging all memory of her illicit passion ('perderà la rimembranza'); the return of these words demonstrates quite the opposite. The clarinet's thrice-repeated, rising 'remembrance' figure in the Adagio section is answered by a similar falling figure in gavotte rhythm at the beginning of the Allegro moderato theme. In both passages the broken declamation reflects Fiordiligi's abject state (see Examples 6.17a–b).

Example 6.17a

Example 6.17b

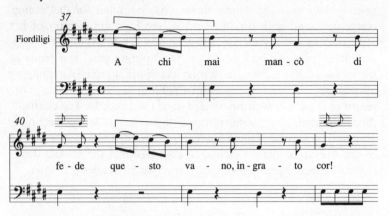

The triadic, horn-like melody of the opening section was model-led on music in *rondòs* Ferrarese had already sung on the stage of the Burgtheater (see Chapter 7), but here two real horns provide obbligato commentary. As Michel Noiray has noted, there was something of a tradition, at least in French opera, of using the horn to represent an absent lover – perhaps on account of associations of posthorns with distance.[29] But Mozart brings the horn calls into ever greater prominence throughout this piece, leaving little doubt, by the end, of their significance as heralds of cuckolding. Strings alone accompany Fiordiligi at first, until bars 8–9, when the suddenly exposed horns (doubled by flutes), give the lie to Fiordiligi's talk of keeping her new flame a secret. In the reprise of the first part Mozart allows the horns and woodwinds to echo the ends of Fiordiligi's phrases, fulfilling their musical potential. The horns come into their own during Fiordiligi's sustained notes in the Allegro moderato, and two previously-heard motifs contribute further referential material. In resetting the line 'perderà la rimembranza' Mozart strays into a paraphrase of the duet 'Prenderò quel brunettino', during which Fiordiligi had unwittingly chosen Ferrando as her suitor; at the start of the coda, a series of rising first-inversion chords decorated with appoggiaturas recalls the central ritornello of Fiordiligi's first aria, thus invoking Guglielmo (see Examples 6.18a–b).[30]

Despite a spectacular cadential flourish, in which the horns parti-cipate fully, it is music associated with Guglielmo that leaves the most lasting impression: Fiordiligi's caressing, *rallentando* cadence phrase in triplets emphasizing the words 'caro bene', and the thrice-repeated figure of Example 6.18b as she leaves the stage.

Example 6.18a

Example 6.18b

Opera buffa models

In line with Mozart's preferences regarding female role-types for an opera buffa (see Chapter 2), Fiordiligi's music in *Così* stands apart from buffa conventions, Dorabella's is *di mezzo carattere*, partaking of both seria (No. 11) and buffa (No. 28) styles, and Despina's is 'entirely buffa'. In writing for the overtly comic characters Mozart relied on prior models no less than in the case of Fiordiligi's music. At the same time, he made Alfonso into a truly original creation, turning the literary saturation of this character's lines, and Bussani's musical limitations, into positive virtues.

Though hardly anything he sings could properly be considered an aria, Alfonso is a dominating figure throughout *Così fan tutte*. His utterances in the first and third trios cause the music to pull up short, reflecting his role as a brake on the folly of his young friends (see Example 6.19).

Example 6.19

Alfonso demonstrates his controlling power also in the Quartetto, No. 22 which, as Tyson has suggested, may originally have been conceived as an aria for him, with echoes by the officers. This ventriloquistic piece (which gives some basis for criticisms of *Così* as a drama of 'marionnettes') constitutes one of Da Ponte's most novel inventions, and Mozart seconds his librettist with a highly witty musical setting. Orchestral phrases depicting the nervous lovers – scored for the unusual combination of upper strings, flutes, and trumpets without timpani – alternate with much suaver material for Alfonso's and (later) Despina's ministrations. Formally, the piece resembles a sonata-rondo without development, in which the secondary theme (bars 12–20) is replaced in the recapitulation by an accompanied recitative for Despina, and the cadence theme (bars

26–36) altered so as to mock the sisters' sighs. The final section presents a Presto, common-time version of the opening motif as Alfonso and Despina leave the stage, singing what for this opera is a rare passage of buffo patter.

Rochlitz calls attention to other memorable moments for Alfonso in ensembles (his 'Saldo amico, finem lauda!' in No. 6, and his 'Misericordia' in the second finale); still more are strewn throughout his recitatives.[31] Both the orchestrally accompanied quotation from Sannazaro and the Ariostan *ottava rima* of No. 30 invited a setting in arioso style. For the latter piece, Alfonso's main statement of principles, Mozart provided music at once flexible and coherent. The severity of the unison phrase 'Tutti accusan le donne' is immediately mitigated by the gently undulating string texture and the suspension on the all-important word 'scuso' (I excuse). A harmonized version of the opening unison gesture (for 'Let others call it a vice') gives way to pseudo-baroque counterpoint in dotted rhythm, illustrating the 'necessity of heart' which leads women to stray. Mozart shows the equivalence of the women's and men's errors through use of similar accompaniments in broken quavers – slurred for the former (bars 3–6), staccato for the latter (12–15). Though the motto begins in unison, as had the initial accusation, Alfonso's reuse of the suspension from bars 4–5 gives it a forgiving tone.

If Alfonso's Nos. 22 and 30 present him at his most original, his first solo number, 'Vorrei dir, e cor non ho' (No. 5), is intentionally derivative. The piece is modelled on 'L'invidia, oh ciel!' in Paisiello's *Il barbiere di Siviglia*, an ironic burst of accompanied recitative within Figaro's narration of his adventures to Count Almaviva. In the Viennese production of Paisiello's opera the role of Figaro was taken by none other than Bussani, the Alfonso of *Così*. Both pieces are in the minor mode, and employ nearly identical accompanimental figurations. But there was an intermediate model for Alfonso's speech, in a miniature aria for Lilla ('Ah pietade, mercede, soccorso') in Da Ponte and Martín's *Una cosa rara*. As in *Così*, the key is F minor, and the talk is specifically about not being able to talk. Da Ponte improves upon his models by making all of Alfonso's stuttering lines end *tronco*. Mozart's refinements include Alfonso's more natural entrance on the dominant, an expanded range of harmonies, and (as noted above) comic extensions of the cadence with syncopations. A further reference in this piece is to *Don Giovanni*: specifically, the death of the Commendatore (played by Bussani, in the 1788 Viennese production), which Mozart quotes almost literally (see Examples 6.20a–b).[32]

Example 6.20a

Example 6.20b

The well-known precedents for 'Vorrei dir' would have helped audiences of *Così* hear Alfonso's outburst as 'rehearsed'.

Perhaps because of the amount of time she spends in disguise, Mozart gave Despina a musical calling-card: a motif in the introduction to her first aria (No. 12) which serves also to identify her upon her appearance as a doctor in the first finale (see Examples 6.21a–b).

The drones and acciaccaturas at the beginning of the aria proper (see Example 6.2b, above) emphasize the folk wisdom in Despina's words, but the musical design of her aria is not without sophistication. The piece is in a compact sonata form, in which the secondary idea of bars 33 ff. returns in a short development section. The reprise of the main theme is to new text: 'O women, let us pay back in like coin this pernicious, indiscreet race of men'; Mozart takes this into account, illustrating this image with a new accompanimental layer of rolling arpeggios and scales in the winds.

Despina's second-act aria, 'Una donna a quindici anni', is complementary in content and form to her first, cataloguing the

Example 6.21a

methods by which women are to repay the opposite sex, and moving
in its two sections from longer to shorter poetic metres. But an even
closer model is to be found in an aria from Da Ponte and Martín's
Una cosa rara, 'Colla flemma che tu vedi', a lesson in the art of
flirtation, sung by Dorothea Bussani – the future Despina – as
Ghita. Da Ponte's intention was clearly to recreate the success of the
earlier number, regardless of his dislike for its singer. In both
Ghita's and Despina's arias *ottonario* and *quinario* lines are juxta-
posed, in sections marked Andante and Allegretto, respectively. The
pieces' concluding sentiments are likewise similar: Ghita asserts that
women are born to be served by men, while Despina says that, like
a queen, a woman must impose obedience. Yet this is not quite the
end in either aria. Lilla comes on, after an apparently final ritornello, and negates Ghita's advice; Despina sings a coda truly regal in
its pretensions, and then repeats an earlier aside to the main
Allegretto theme (teasingly anticipated by the orchestra). In terms of
musical substance, 'Una donna a quindici anni' owes little to
Martín's aria, beyond its use of 6/8 metre. Mozart is far more successful in imparting an air of coquetry, by means of coy inflections

Example 6.21b

and silences in Despina's melody, and by suggestive flute-and-bassoon doublings.

Guglielmo's 'Non siate ritrosi' shares several features with the aria just described, including its key, its prominent use of flute and bassoon, even its suggestive uses of the *Così*-trill (found also in his rejected aria). Guglielmo's other aria, 'Donne mie', was worked out

Example 6.22a

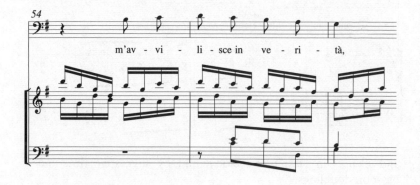

Example 6.22b

with unusual care by Mozart (sketch material survives). The aria's principal material is not so much a theme as an orchestral transition (initially, out of the preceding recitative). The horn-calls accompanying Guglielmo's statement of 'Donne mie, la fate a tanti' clarify at once the significance of just what women do so much to men, but this material did not bear repeating exactly. Accordingly, Da Ponte varied the wording in each subsequent recurrence, prefacing each with a 'ma' (but) which erases Guglielmo's intervening protestations of goodwill towards women. Mozart sets the refrain as a downward spiral of thirds over a dominant seventh, elaborated by the violins in a semiquaver motif suggesting the 'tanti e tanti' on whose behalf Guglielmo complains. For its final occurrence, Mozart extends the accompanying figure and makes it canonic, in a feverish, dissonant intensification of the accusation (see Examples 6.22a–b).

The material of the episodes is richly allusive: orchestral *révérences* at bars 41–3 demonstrating 'marks of friendship', military sounds at 'Mille volte il brando presi' and, as an illustration of the treasures poured down on women by heaven (bars 93 ff.), a figure Mozart had used at the text 'Et misericordia' in the 'Magnificat' of his 'Vesperæ solennes de confessore', K339. Guglielmo's – and Dorabella's – uncomplicated nature is evident also in the relatively straightforward plan and material of the duet in which he seduces her. From the start, both sing similar material, and they move so quickly to parallel singing that the outcome of their encounter seems a foregone conclusion. During a brief development section (bars 48–68) Dorabella offers scarcely any resistance as Guglielmo replaces Ferrando's portrait in her locket with his heart. The recapitulation – and her surrender – are announced before either singer utters a word, by a horn-call version of her first phrase (rather than Guglielmo's) from the main theme. They combine their voices in sweet tenths in the final section of the duet, which begins with a delightfully over-obvious depiction by the first violins of the 'happy exchange of hearts and affections', based on the motif that had accompanied Guglielmo's actions during the middle section (see Examples 6.23a–b). The lovers end by singing of 'new delights' – paradoxically, to a version of Guglielmo's very first phrase.

By contrast, Fiordiligi and Ferrando's duet (No. 29) is much more fraught with tensions and ironies, and the structure which articulates them is more complicated. There are hardly any returns of material; rather, the characters reach outside of the piece to prior music. Singing a duet is the furthest thing from Fiordiligi's mind as

Example 6.23a

Example 6.23b

she begins what the spectators, too, assume to be an aria, and once Ferrando surprises her, she does her utmost to repel him, with repeated imperatives ('. . .deh partite!', 'Taci. . . ahimè', 'Sorgi'). Her inability to control the situation is evident in the duet's construction as a series of interrupted and uncompleted periods. Ferrando completes Fiordiligi's modulation to the dominant, but changes the mode to minor; later, after she has landed with an anguished cry on the dominant of A minor (bars 74–5), he switches mode, metre and tempo. Though the original tonic returns at the start of Ferrando's Larghetto (see Example 6.14a above), its preparation has not been sufficient to lend this moment the feeling of a resolution. After sixteen bars Fiordiligi jumps in with another exclamation, prompting Ferrando to perservere. As she helplessly echoes his phrases, Ferrando, assisted by the oboe, then guides the melody to the upper tonic and a cadence which seals his victory. The cadence at the start of the final Andante section *a 2* is marked by the return of a motif that had originally illustrated the embraces Fiordiligi had hoped to share with Guglielmo; here, as Guglielmo watches in agony from the wings, it signifies the embraces of Fiordiligi and Ferrando (see Examples 6.24a–b).

Final games

In describing the typical finale of an opera buffa, Da Ponte emphasized not advancement or resolution of the plot, but rather effects calculated to build to a rousing conclusion. A finale was to be 'a sort of miniature comedy [commediola]', with its own new subplot. Here it was 'the genius of the composer, the force of the singers' which had to shine, the poet's main task being to find opportunities for every conceivable combination of voices and type of motion and emotion, from adagio to 'strepitosissimo'.[33] In order to satisfy the requirement of a separate intrigue, many librettists had recourse to disguises, and to language that was overtly theatrical. By these criteria, the two finales of *Così fan tutte* have been judged to be classic examples. In a drama already centrally concerned with disguise, Despina's masquerades as a doctor and a notary heightened this aspect to the point of absurdity. The characters themselves call attention to the artifice of the first finale: no 'finer comedy' (più bella commediola) than the sisters' distress was to be found, declare the poisoned Albanians, *a parte*, no 'more hilarious a picture', say all the schemers towards the end. The final gesture of the act is a chromatically rising crescendo which paints the very word 'cresce', in the sisters' threats of dire consequences 'if my rage grows any further'.

The soldiers' first essay of their Albanian disguises elicited a finale-like response from Mozart and his librettist, in the multisectional sextet, No. 13. The two-bar orchestral introduction archly cites the music of 'Andiam, andiam, mio bene' (from *Don Giovanni*),

Example 6.24a

Fiordiligi

Fra gli am - ples - si   in po - chi i-stan - ti   giun - ge - rò del fi - do spo - so;

in march rhythm,[34] signalling the Albanians' intentions. The sextet is a kind of rehearsal for the first finale: the 'poison' here is drunk by the women, in the form of unanticipated amorous stimulation; the men's closing comments on the ambiguity of the sisters' rage are hardly different from those at the end of the act. Of central importance in the sextet are the mock-pathetic pleadings in A minor before the sisters by the kneeling Ferrando and Guglielmo, and Despina, on their behalf (bars 82–103). Not only the extravagant language of these 'spasimanti adorator', but also the Neapolitan harmony and part-writing in mirror-image (inverted upon repetition) betray the underlying parody (see Example 6.25).[35]

The uses of sonata form in the larger ensembles of Mozart's operas have been given considerable emphasis in the analytical literature, but the principle of alternating periods of action and expression is rather more significant in the working-out of his act-finales. As described by John Platoff, Viennese finales usually consist of a succession of musico-dramatic units, articulated by tonality,

Example 6.24b

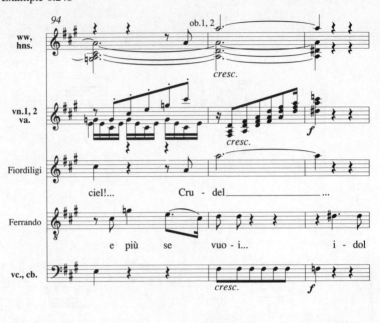

setting, entrances and exits of characters, or poetic metre, in each of which an action is usually followed by a passage of reflection.[36] In the first finale, the sections are disposed as shown in Table 6.2:

Table 6.2: *Structure of Finale I*

bars	characters	key	metre	tempo	text incipit	poetic metre	A/E
1	Fi, Do	D	2/4	Andante	Ah che tutto in un momento	8	E
62	+ Fe, G, A	g	¢	Allegro	Si mora, sì, si mora	7	A
112					Ah che del sole il raggio		E
138	(+ D)	E♭			Giacchè a morir vicini	7	A
198	– D, A				Dei che cimento è questo		E
218		c			Ah! / Sospiran gl'infelici	8	A
267					Più domestiche e trattabili		E
292	+ D, A	G	3/4	Allegro	Eccovi il medico	5	A
418					Attorno guardano		E
		///					
429		B♭	C	Andante	Dove son, che loco è questo	8	A/E (mixed)
		///					
485		D	¢	Allegro	Dammi un bacio o mio tesoro	8	A/E (mixed)
544					Un quadretto più giocondo		

The tonal moves by third into the last two sections – hardly typical of sonata form – show the disorientation of the men upon 'awakening', and the women's surprise at their request for a kiss. These and the men's other actions in this finale are in jest; the main interest lies instead in the actions of the women, which are at their most revealing in the development-like section after Despina's departure in search of aid (bars 218 ff.). Over the peregrinations of two orchestral motifs, the first of which illustrates the poisoned strangers' heartbeats, Fiordiligi and Dorabella draw ever closer to the suitors they believe to be unconscious, eventually even feeling their foreheads and pulses. They revert to their former outrage after the men return to their senses, but in the 'expression' passage of this unit Ferrando and Guglielmo note *sotto voce* that their fiancées have become alarmingly amenable.

Mozart seized gleefully on the farcical aspects of Despina's appearance as doctor: her parade of languages, ostentatiously methodical examination (reflected in the motific single-mindedness of the music)

Example 6.25

and her magnetic cure. The composer illustrates Despina's initial ministrations with a violin figure in mirror-image (bars 327 and 330), and later demonstrates the magnet's power (bars 361–9) by effecting an impressive modulation, *crescendo*, to the keynote of the opera. But equally farcical is the music of the poisoning, which dispels so suddenly the torpor of the sisters' lamentations. Mozart set this entire section in the dire key of G minor, though with the key signature of G major throughout. Various explanations have been offered of this notational quirk, which cost the copyists much extra effort.[37] The simplest is probably that, this being a *mock*-suicide scene, G major is only worn as a mask – as an inside joke for the musicians themselves. Here, as in Fiordiligi's first aria, Mozart uses B♭ trumpets without timpani, mainly for *forte* blasts on their third degree (the dominant of G minor). The women's horrified reactions to the pisoning ('Il tragico spettacolo / Gelare il cor mi fa!'; bars 89 ff.) show the influence of Alfonso's earlier play-acting in No. 5 (see Example 6.20b, above). A sequence featuring five augmented triads, both accented and passing, comically illustrates the 'disperato affetto' which drove the Albanians to suicide (see Example 6.26).

Example 6.26

The second finale starts out on a similar trajectory from stasis (preparations for the marriage ceremony) to surprise and distress (the soldiers' return), again with opportunity for a *tour de force* by Despina. But in this finale the librettist and composer had also to negotiate the journey from shame and anger to reconciliation. Though the soldiers had apparently accepted Alfonso's advice to 'take them as they are', and pronounced themselves 'contentissimi' with the planned wedding charade, the canonic toast proves a formidable obstacle. Not only does Guglielmo choke on its words, but the very beauty of its music sets a high standard for that of the dénouement, once the original pairings have been restored.

The untying of the new nuptial knot begins as a rather grim farce (following Alfonso's 'Misericordia'), with a reversion to the sorts of

Example 6.27

sounds that had accompanied the mock-poisoning. At bars 357–9 the sisters employ the same melodic figure and harmony as at 'Gelare il cor mi fa!' in the first finale, again to stereotypical expressions of consternation. The soldiers' eruption of fury on discovering the wedding contract is pure show (see Example 6.11b), and their fiancées' initial acknowledgement of guilt is less than entirely convincing – sung, as it is, to a version of the officers' music at 'Sani e salvi', and admixed with blame for Alfonso and 'the seductress'. Only after the philosopher explains the symmetry of the lesson (see Example 6.10) does their remorse – expressed in drooping phrases that incorporate both Alfonso's descending fourth and a slowed-down *Così*-trill – seem sincere (see Example 6.27).

Fermatas at the ends of their phrases add weight to the passage, but also allow for expansion upon repetition, as their fiancés' and Despina's comments are fitted in underneath. (Despina's philosophical comment 'So much the better if they've done it to me, for I do it to many others' in bars 565–7 – yet another version of the opera's motto – is set to essentially the same music as Alfonso's phrase 'Che vi sia ciascun lo dice' in No. 2.) The music leading up to the final Allegro molto is satisfying also on account of its pedals and drastically slower harmonic motion, and because, in contrast to the first finale, Mozart here provides a thorough preparation for the tonic's return. The keynote appears briefly with the recall of Despina's Mesmerian cure; Mozart then retreats to A minor and its dominant, from which he methodically approaches C major through the circle of fifths.

True to form, the final tutti begins and ends with allusions to earlier music. The opening wind phrases recall the music to 'Così ognor quest'alma è forte' in Fiordiligi's No. 14 – auguring well for the couples' future,[38] while the string figures of the postlude quote from Guglielmo's No. 26, as a rejoinder (see Examples 6.28a–b).[39]

In between, Mozart's music paints the 'whirlwinds of this world' (as well as laughter and weeping) more than the 'serenity' provided by reason, but this was inevitable, given the requirements of a *stretta*. For 'bella calma' one must look instead to the preceding section.

Is this music sufficient for a resolution? Many have argued that it is not, but Frits Noske rightly observes that the text of the reconciliation in *Le nozze di Figaro* is at least as banal as that in *Così*, and much shorter besides. To be fair to both works, one must remember that 'Da Ponte did not write a drama but rather provided the composer with material for a drama.'[40] And while one may wonder

Example 6.28a

Example 6.28b

how long Fiordiligi will remain satisfied with the return to the status quo, such thoughts should not spoil our pleasure in the opera any more than in the case of the Countess. Within the bounds prescribed by the eighteenth-century comic tradition, Da Ponte, and Mozart in particular, have brought this drama to a satisfactory resolution.

We conclude with the Overture, the composition of which Mozart habitually saved until last. Several generations of listeners have been puzzled by this piece, probably the closest Mozart ever came to composing in *grisaille*. The sense of the framing motto was clear enough, as commentators from Rochlitz onwards have attested, and the theme's near-quotation of Basilio's line 'Così fan tutte le belle' in *Le nozze di Figaro* cannot long have remained unnoticed (see Examples 1.1a–b).[41] Rather, it was Mozart's 'deliberately empty and commonplace' material which demanded to be explained.[42] Tovey described the Overture as 'one of the funniest things Mozart ever wrote', its themes demonstrating that the characters 'are, humanly speaking, rubbish, but far too harmless for any limbo less charitable than the eternal laughter of Mozart'.[43] Ulybyshev before him assert-ed that the constant trading of motifs between wind instruments in the Presto represented the '*génie féminin*. . .constancy in inconstancy alone'.[44] This analogy can be pursued in some detail, for not only do all three parts of the theme include the *Così*-trill in one form or another (see Example 6.29a–b, and 6.1b above), but the order in which the wind instruments enter with their circling motif, singly or in pairs, is varied throughout the course of the movement, only to be restored at the recapitulation.

Example 6.29a

Example 6.29b

The bassoon leads off in the statement which begins the development section at bar 79; the clarinet does so in a subdominant statement at bar 148. In a restatement at bb. 157 ff. the solo winds double each other in octaves throughout, for the first time in the movement; this transgression is seemingly punished by the entrance, *forte*, of the syncopated tutti phrase, which moves through D minor and then the minor tonic to a retransition over a dominant pedal. Although the four solo winds cannot be equated in literal fashion with the four lovers, their combinations and recombinations would surely be suggestive for spectators acquainted with the premise of the opera.

Structurally, too, the Overture contains clues as to the nature of the drama to come. Mozart's placement of Alfonso's motto at both its beginning and end reflects the philosopher's words of very similar advice to his friends at the beginning of the action, and again near the conclusion, after they have had the experience necessary to appreciate his advice – the Presto section of the Overture representing that experience. And the composer's reuse at the end of the Overture of the last five bars of the second finale, practically unaltered, was calculated subliminally to reinforce (when heard in proper succession) the spectators' perception of all the work's symmetries – of cast, plot, moral and music – as the very last impression they received.

7 *Performance and criticism*

The first interpreters

The singers who first performed Mozart's *Così fan tutte* were not uniformly committed to the success of the opera, or of its authors. Francesco Bussani and his wife Dorothea (née Sardi) were openly antagonistic to Da Ponte, who (so they thought) had unfairly denied them leading roles. Adriana Ferrarese and Louise Villeneuve, both relative newcomers to the troupe, were equally vexatious, as we have seen. The one veteran whom Mozart could count as an ally was the *primo buffo* Francesco Benucci, the first Figaro and Guglielmo, and the first Viennese Leporello. It was perhaps out of gratitude to him that Mozart composed the grandly proportioned aria 'Rivolgete a lui lo sguardo', a dramatic miscalculation which Mozart eventually saw fit to sacrifice.

Benucci had already been partnered with Nancy Storace before being recruited for the Viennese opera buffa company.[1] Though both were talented singers, it was in large part the naturalness of their acting – refined through close observation of performances in the German-language Nationaltheater – that distinguished them from their colleagues.[2] Michael Kelly, another member of the original troupe, wrote in later years of witnessing Mozart's immense satisfaction with Benucci's performance of 'Non più andrai, farfallone amoroso' in *Figaro*, and particularly of 'the fine passage "Cherubino, alla vittoria, alla gloria militar," which he gave out with Stentorian lungs'.[3] In *Così* Mozart sought even to surpass this effect, with the ringing triadic cadences of the aria Benucci was to have sung in Act I, which repeatedly carried him to a high F♯ (see Example 7.1).

This piece also allowed the singer to display his gifts for parody and innuendo (the opening section), for buffo patter ('In amor i Marcantoni / Verso noi sarian buffoni', bars 79–85), even his ability to trill (see Example 7.2).

Example 7.1

Example 7.2

Though in the end deprived of this showpiece, Benucci was given ample opportunity for showmanship in its self-descriptive replacement, 'Non siate ritrosi'. Considering that he is one of the opera's four lovers, Guglielmo/Benucci has remarkably little amorous-sounding music, even in his love duet with Dorabella, which relies instead on such opera-buffa clichés as the depiction of the lovers' heartbeats. In Benucci's final aria, 'Donne mie, la fate a tanti', there were constant invitations to the comic actor, in the piece's many 'ma's and ambiguous 'perchè's.

Playing Fiordiligi to Benucci's Guglielmo was a singer of quite opposite temperament, the soprano Adriana Ferrarese del Bene. There has been considerable confusion regarding this singer's identity, ever since the music biographer Ernst Ludwig Gerber confused her with a Francesca Gabrielli, called 'la Ferrarese' after her birthplace, whom Charles Burney had heard in Venice in 1770.[4] 'Ferrarese' (or 'Ferraresi') seems to have been the singer's surname, and not a descriptive stage-name.[5] Trained in the sacred repertory at the Mendicanti in Venice, Ferrarese graduated to leading roles in opera seria, which remained her preference even though circumstances required her to take roles in opera buffa in both London and Vienna. Even in this latter repertory, she insisted on singing parts that were mostly or entirely serious. And when taking over a role created by another singer, as in her 1788 Viennese début as the eponymous goddess of Martín's *L'arbore di Diana*, she demanded extensive revisions and additions to her music, in order to show her voice to best effect.[6] The music-loving Count Zinzendorf was favourably impressed by Ferrarese, but Emperor Joseph was less enthusiastic. 'As far as I can recall la Ferraresi', he wrote to his opera director, 'she has a rather weak contralto voice, knows music very well, but has a rather ugly figure.'[7] The anonymous author of the 1790 pamphlet *Grundsätze zur Theaterkritik*, while granting that she possessed a varied and 'unusual' voice, criticized her acting, in particular – and quite possibly in connection with *Così* – her tendency to forget 'the respect due a worthy audience' when portraying anger on the stage.[8] Even Da Ponte, who was otherwise partial to her, had to admit that 'she was not the best of actresses; but with two most beautiful eyes, and a very fair mouth, few were the operas in which she did not please infinitely'.[9] Mozart, usually a good judge of vocal and dramatic talent, doubted Ferrarese's ability to sing with sufficient naïveté the aria 'Un moto di gioia' (K579) that he had composed for her performance (replacing Storace) in *Le nozze di Figaro* in August of 1789.[10] But with the other new piece for Susanna – a showpiece *rondò* ('Al desio di chi t'adora', K577) for the tryst scene in the garden – the composer played to her strengths, as he would also in creating for her the role of Fiordiligi.

The two-tempo *rondò* was a type of piece with which Ferrarese was particularly associated, both before and after her arrival in Vienna. As the climactic solo number for an opera's heroine (or hero, if a castrato), it was invariably preceded by an imposing accompanied recitative; its opening slow section and faster second part provided opportunities for affective singing and brilliant coloratura, respectively. As John Rice has noted, the three *rondò*s written for Ferrarese by Mozart and Salieri – 'Al desio' in *Figaro*, 'Sola e mesta fra tormenti' in the latter's *La cifra* of December 1789, and 'Per pietà, ben mio, perdona' in *Così* – show these two composers vying with each other to produce ever more effective vehicles for this soprano. From one *rondò* to the next, the vocal range covered expands in either direction, while scalar passages, triplet roulades and leaps between registers are deployed in increasing abundance (see Example 7.3).[11]

Example 7.3

There is a more substantive link as well: the horn-harmonies which hint openly at cuckoldry at the opening of 'Al desio' were imitated – without this dramatic justification – in 'Sola e mesta' (likewise in F major), and appear again in 'Per pietà', with all their connotations intact.

The qualities that suited Ferrarese to the prime roles in the Viennese repertory – her agility in passage-work and powerful lower register – left her prone to mockery, as when Mozart gives her a burst of coloratura in a thick ensemble texture (No. 13, Finale I), or exaggerated leaps between registers in inappropriate situations (before and during 'Come scoglio'). These talents also made her the object of the jealousy of other sopranos in the troupe: of Salieri's protégée Catarina Cavalieri (Franziska Kavalier), and of Dorothea Bussani.[12] On the other hand, no enmity is known to have existed between Ferrarese and Louise Villeneuve, the first Dorabella, whose voice was darker, lower in tessitura, and generally less agile than hers. But neither is there any evidence – apart from an unsupported assertion by Haydn's biographer Carl Friedrich Pohl – that the two singers were sisters in real life.[13] Villeneuve was probably the younger of the two; in the *Grundsätze zur Theaterkritik* she is called 'a young girl, pleasant to look at, [who] sings not badly, as long as she stays in tune'.[14] Mozart refers to her in his letters as 'Louise' rather than 'Luisa' Villeneuve, though it is unclear how far back were her French origins; before coming to Vienna she was active at the Teatro San Moisè in Venice.[15] Although Villeneuve had not yet participated in one of Mozart's own operas, she was the recipient of three insertion arias from his pen: 'Alma grande e nobil core' (K578) – an indignant defence against an unjust accusation of infidelity – in Cimarosa's *I due baroni di Rocca Azzura*; and 'Chi sa, chi sa qual sia' and 'Vado, ma dove?' (K582 and 583) in Martín's *Il burbero di buon cuore*.

The good humour of Villeneuve's aria 'È Amore un ladroncello' was an element mostly absent from Fiordiligi's role. Musically, too, the singers were clearly differentiated. Whereas Ferrarese was at ease with rapid passage-work, Villeneuve was more comfortable with triadic writing, which predominates in both of her arias in *Così*. Though Mozart gave the women equivalent melismas in their two duets, such figures are entirely lacking in Dorabella's solo numbers, and in the larger ensembles as well, where Ferrando alone responds in kind to Fiordiligi's outbursts. Though it was rumoured early in 1791 that the new emperor, Leopold II, had fallen in love with Villeneuve, she was let go before the beginning of the next opera season.[16]

The original Ferrando, Vincenzo Calvesi, was a singer of relatively long standing with the Viennese opera buffa company, having arrived in 1785 from Venice; his début was as Sandrino in Paisiello's *Il re Teodoro in Venezia*. His 'extraordinarily beautiful voice',[17] more even than that of Adriana Ferrarese, put its imprint on the music of *Così*, starting in the second measure of its overture, with an overflowing lyric phrase such as he sings at several points in the drama (see Examples 7.4a–e).

Calvesi played not only the lyric lover, but also an ardent one, in 'Ah! lo veggio, quell'anima bella', No. 24. The fiendish difficulty of this forward-pressing rondo, in which Ferrando is called upon to sing thirteen high B♭s, has long been explained in terms of its instrumental origins, in a fragmentary movement for clarinet quintet, K581a. But Alan Tyson has suggested that this fragment, with its thirteen changes of clef in the clarinet part within the space of nineteen bars, was not a projected finale for the Quintet K580, as has been surmised, but rather 'that it was intended for domestic amusement, perhaps even for the discomfiture of his friend Anton

Example 7.4a: Overture

Example 7.4b: No. 3

Example 7.4c: No. 6

Example 7.4d: No. 29

Example 7.4e: No. 29

Stadler, and is thus more likely to have been written after the opera than before it.'[18] Given that 'Ah! lo veggio' was cut by the composer before or during the first production,[19] one might be tempted to think that Mozart's reuse of its melody in the quintet movement was a joke at his own expense, on account of the aria's difficulty. But given that Mozart was already acquainted with Calvesi's voice, it seems possible that his decision to remove the aria stemmed in part from dramaturgical considerations: Ferrando's overexposure in Act II, or a desire not to upstage Fiordiligi's *rondò*.

Paradoxically, the only unattached characters in *Così* were played by the married couple of Dorothea and Francesco Bussani. Da

Ponte, no friend of either of them, turned the twenty-year difference between their ages into a joke, when Despina tells Alfonso that 'an old man like you cannot do anything to a girl'. The Roman-born Francesco was a member of the Viennese opera buffa troupe from its foundation in 1783, and had created the Mozartian roles of Bartolo and Antonio in *Le nozze di Figaro*, doubling also those of the Commendatore and Masetto in the Vienna production of *Don Giovanni*. He had styled himself a *primo buffo* while still in Italy, but in Vienna he had to relinquish such ambitions in the face of Benucci's superior talents.[20] Besides singing, Bussani was also active as a stage manager, and in this capacity he (reportedly) nearly derailed preparations for *Le nozze di Figaro*, with his officious objections to the ballet scene in Act III.[21] Whatever his musical shortcomings, Da Ponte and Mozart took full advantage of Bussani's gifts as an actor. His 'joking' quotation of Metastasio in No. 2, his false grief in No. 5, and false surprise at the appearance of the Albanians and later upon the return of his soldier friends, and his benevolent chiding in No. 30 – all are dependent on the surest instincts of timing and tone, for which even the most precise notation was no substitute.

Bussani's wife Dorothea was the only native-born Viennese in the cast of the opera. She too had pretensions to better roles than she was given – though these included such plums as Cherubino. Da Ponte twice derides her in his memoirs, in nearly identical terms, as a singer who, 'though vulgar and of little merit, by dint of grimaces, of buffoonery and perhaps also of more theatrical means [i.e. amorous liaisons]. . . still managed to gain a great following among the cooks, footmen, servants, lackeys, wigmakers, etc.'[22] If there were only a portion of truth in this portrayal, it would still give an ironic resonance to Despina's complaints about life as a servant, in her first appearance in *Così*. 'Grimaces' and 'buffoonery' abound in the music for Despina in her guises as doctor and notary, but her two arias confirm that Bussani possessed a 'beautiful and graceful chest voice'[23] and, in her phrases beginning 'E qual regina' in No. 19, aspirations to better things.

The myth of the failed première.

Così fan tutte had been given five times by the time the death of Joseph II on 20 February 1790 put a halt to performances in all of Vienna's theatres. There were five further performances during the summer, and thereafter the opera was not heard in the Austrian capital until 1794, when it was given in German at the Theater an der Wien (in K. L. Gieseke's translation). That *Così* was not a success is implied rather than stated outright in most modern accounts; such a conclusion would seem reasonable, given the tremendous popularity of *Figaro* and, at least in Prague, of *Don Giovanni*. The long runs in Vienna of such operas as *L'arbore di Diana* and *Una cosa rara* (40 and 26 performances, respectively, during the years 1789–91), likewise dwarf the meagre totals for *Così fan tutte*. The single mention of the première of *Così* in the Viennese press is strictly factual, but another report, in the Weimar *Journal des Luxus und der Moden*, is entirely favourable:

I announce to you another excellent work of Mozart that our theatre has received. Yesterday, to wit, it was given for the first time in the I[mperial] R[oyal] National-Theatre. It has the title: Cosi fan tutte, o sia, la Scuola degli Amanti. The text is by the Abbate Da Ponte, poet of the Italian opera in the I[mperial] R[oyal] court theatre. Concerning the music: that it is by Mozart says all, I believe.[24]

Count Carl von Zinzendorf, an indefatigable if not always perceptive spectator, noted in his diary following a performance of the opera on 26 January that 'Mozart's music is charming, and the subject rather amusing.'[25] (Vincent Novello, having solicited Constanze Mozart's opinion of the opera nearly three decades after the première, reported that 'She does not much admire the plot of 'Così fan', but agreed with me that such music would carry any piece through. . .'[26]) New archival evidence brought to light by Dexter Edge shows that this première was in fact the most heavily attended opera performance of the entire 1789/90 season; the average of box-office receipts for all operatic performances also puts Mozart's work in the lead.[27] Edge rightly points out that the period of mourning for Joseph II was followed immediately by the usual Lenten closure of all theatres; thereafter, pieces already in the repertory took a back seat to works conceived for the new season. The delay in reviving *Così fan tutte* is likewise explicable in terms of changing patronage. The new emperor Leopold II, after first attending to the dire political situation he had inherited from his brother, set about in 1791 fundamentally to change the direction of Viennese operatic life. He fired Da Ponte and many others in the company (including Ferrarese), and introduced a repertory in which opera seria and ballet were dominant. His preference in opera buffa – epitomized by the works of Cimarosa – was for a form radically simpler than that cultivated by Mozart during the previous decade.[28] Under such circumstances, and especially with Da Ponte's rival Bertati now installed as theatre poet, it was hardly likely that *Così* would be revived by the new opera company.

Another index of the popularity of *Così fan tutte* in Vienna is the publication during 1790 by Artaria of excerpts from Mozart's score. The first piece to be advertised, on 20 February (the very day of the emperor's death), was 'that most beautiful duetto: Il Core vi dono bel Idolo mio' (No. 23); the other numbers to appear were the overture; the duets Nos. 4, 7 and 20; the march 'Bella vita militar', No. 8; and the arias Nos. 15, 19 and 28 for Guglielmo, Despina and Dorabella, respectively.[29] The absence of Fiordiligi's two arias is perhaps due to their technical difficulty; more difficult to explain is that of 'Smanie implacabili', which presents no such obstacles to the amateur performer.

The fortunes of *Così* to 1848

During the period roughly from the French Revolution to the revolutions of 1848, *Così fan tutte* lagged well behind Mozart's other mature operas, in terms of both performance statistics and the sympathy of critics. Though none of these works were exempt from the tampering of translators and arrangers (as they still are not), *Così* was especially prone to distortions, which occasionally reflected the social and political issues of the times. Yet the post-Mozartian history of the opera is not entirely a catalogue of horrors, for there were still pockets of understanding long after Mozart's death.

In the wake of the Viennese première there were a few original-language productions of *Così* in German-speaking Europe, but these fell far short of presenting the opera in an authentic form. During 1791, Prague, Leipzig and Dresden saw a version staged by Domenico Guardasoni, successor to the Pasquale Bondini whose company had first given *Don Giovanni* in 1787. Antonio Baglioni, who had created the Mozartian roles of Don Ottavio and Tito with this troupe, was chided in 1794 (possibly with reference to this 1791 production) for being unable to 'cope with his arias in Mozart's *Così fan tutte*'.[30] This is not surprising, given Baglioni's tessitura, so low that Němetschek referred to him as a 'mezzo basso'. Judging from the Dresden libretto, Bondini's production was savagely cut; a third of the set pieces were eliminated or converted into recitative. The simple recitatives, too, were abridged, eliminating much of the piece's equivocal content. Dresden was still hearing Mozart's operas in Italian during the Napoleonic era, but rarely. 'Though the performance came off well indeed', a critic reported on the occasion of an 1812 revival, 'the house remained mostly empty through three performances!'[31] (Around this same time, Cimarosa's *Il matrimonio segreto* had reached its 150th performance there.) In a more detailed report from Dresden two years later, Mozart's score for *Così* is called

this heavenly music, here (would one believe it?) formerly scorned. . ., [this] abundant fund of the most beautiful melodies, of the most select harmonies, in equal measure original and yet natural, ingenious and yet comprehensible, extremely diverse and yet most closely bound together as a whole, full of hilarity and humour, without a trace of frivolity or vulgarity.[32]

The writer credits Da Ponte only grudgingly with having provided 'a certain theatrical-musical routine' susceptible of a good musical setting. The review ends with criticism of the men's 'inappropriate' disguise as Hussars, effusive praise for the great precision of the orchestra, and the wish for a larger place for Mozart in the repertory.

Così was slow to arrive in Italy (where it was usually known as *La scuola degli amanti*). It was apparently heard first in Trieste in 1797, in a performance featuring Adriana Ferrarese, and then not until 1805, at Varese. The opera's Milanese première took place at La Scala two years later. Though generally considered to be exceedingly difficult, Mozart's operas did eventually come to be appreciated on the Italian peninsula. Philip Gossett has written of almost reciprocal influences between *Così* and *Il turco in Italia*, another 'comedy of manners, whose themes of disguise and of the boundaries between reality and imagination seem peculiarly modern'. In its first incarnation, with a libretto by Da Ponte's patron Caterino Mazzolà, *Il turco* had reached the stage of the Viennese Burgtheater during the summer of 1789, just as Da Ponte was drafting his text to *Così*; as adapted by Felice Romani, the work was set to music by Rossini during a long series of performances of *Così* (again, massively cut) at La Scala in Milan in 1814. Two singers from the production became principals in Rossini's opera.[33] *Così fan tutte* received its French première in the original language, in 1809, but the opera was nonetheless cruelly mutilated by cuts, retextings, and reassignment of pieces. The first performance in French of music from *Così*, four years later, was in a pasticcio on a new libretto altogether, in which many persons had a hand.[34]

It was primarily in German translation that *Così fan tutte* entered the repertory in the decades following its première. The literature on the opera is replete with condemnations of the liberties taken with Da Ponte's text in the various adaptations that came into circulation after 1790. But whatever their deficiencies, these arrangements for a mostly bourgeois audience enabled a fairly wide diffusion for *Così*, which it would not have enjoyed in its original form.[35]

The earliest translation of *Così* seems to have been that of Wenzel Mihule for the 1790/91 season of the Vaterländisches Theater in Prague.[36] In common with subsequent translators, Mihule faced the problem of what to call this opera, whose original title said little to an audience ignorant of Italian. He simply translated literally both the title (*Eine machts wie die andere*) and subtitle, but other adaptors sought to find an equivalently proverbial German expression – the most felicitous being Christoph Friedrich Bretzner's *Weibertreue, oder die Mädchen sind von Flandern* (1794, for Leipzig).[37] Though varying in details, most early adaptations were alike in certain fundamental respects. The Neapolitan setting was usually dropped, and characters' names were often Germanicized, or changed altogether.[38] In conformity with normal German practice, all simple recitative was reworked as spoken dialogue. Da Ponte was only rarely named as the original author, which encouraged a certain leeway on the part of translators, who also borrowed freely from each other's versions.

With its many topical and literary references, the text of *Così fan tutte* was particularly prone to distortion when translated. Operatic diction and quotations were routinely suppressed, and alternatives found for some of Da Ponte's more idiomatic expressions. As Despina spouts legalistic jargon in her guise as notary in the second finale, for instance, Mihule has her formally wish the new couples 'happiness and blessings', and works in a Latin phrase which in effect recommends a form of birth control:

> *Ad obsequia* Ihro Gnaden!
> Hier bin ich von Amteswegen.
> Wünsch im Voraus Glük und Seegen,
> *Interrupta gaudia.*

Bretzner, apparently aware that 'È la fede delle femmine' was an operatic quotation, replaced it with an allusion to a work quoted in *Don Giovanni*, which his audience would be more likely to recognize:

Weibertreu ist *Cosa rara*,
Ist der ächte Stein der Weisen. . .

(The fidelity of women is *cosa rara*, the true philosopher's
stone. . .)

At *Così*'s Viennese première, the men had gone off to fight an
unnamed enemy, but Bretzner's Alfonso of 1794 specifies: 'They
have to go off to war, against the French!' Accordingly, in No. 13
Despina no longer takes the suitors to be Wallachian or Turkish,
but instead asks 'Sind's Husaren, sind's Polacken, / Oder sind es
Sansculots?'[39] But even while preserving the allusiveness of the
original, Bretzner skewed some of its most essential themes. In No.
4, at the point where the sisters had called upon Cupid to punish
them should they ever stray, Bretzner has them voice their worries
about their fiancé's wandering eyes. In the second finale, the men do
not acknowledge learning any lesson; instead of renouncing further
proofs, they declare that their test of the women had merely been
a joke. A further gesture towards accommodating the sensibilities
of female spectators was Bretzner's addition of a second, 'parody'
strophe for Guglielmo's aria 'Donne mie, la fate a tanti', in which
the Flanders-proverb is directed against men:

Mädchen, Engel seyd Ihr alle,
Wie ein Täubchen sanft und schön,
Aber Schelme sind wir alle,
Listig euch zu hintergehn.
. . . .
Ach! wir alle sind von Flandern,
Küssen da, und küssen dort;
Froh zu tändeln, leicht zu wandern,
Bricht man Treue, Schwur und Wort. . .

(Ladies, all of you are angels, soft and fair as doves, but we
men are all scoundrels for slyly deceiving you. . .Ah! we're all
from Flanders, kissing here and kissing there; glad to dally,
quick to stray, breaking faith, vow and word. . .)[40]

Critical reactions to *Così fan tutte* during its first decades on the
German stage range from out-of-hand condemnation to enthusiastic
appreciation of the work's irony and delicacy of nuance. In 1794,
the actor Friedrich Ludwig Schröder called Frankfurt's *Liebe und
Versuchung* (Love and temptation, by H. G. Schmieder and C. D.
Stegmann) 'a miserable thing, which denigrates all women, cannot
possibly please female spectators and therefore will have no success'.[41]

Goethe's mother called this same adaptation 'abominable', and in 1797 requested that her son – then theatre intendant in Weimar – send a new version (by her son-in-law, Christian August Vulpius) that had been given there, by which the opera had 'gained immensely'.[42] Rochlitz, writing in 1801, blamed *Così*'s unpopularity on the nature of the German audience itself:

The German public has altogether too much heaviness and too little frivolity of temperament for this sort of comedy; and most of our singers are not nearly good enough actors, and above all not refined, droll or roguish enough for this type of Italian burlesque, when it is pushed as far as it is here.[43]

Only if a German poet provided a new text for Mozart's music, he wrote, could a German public readily accept the opera. A critic writing for the *Allgemeine musikalische Zeitung* in March 1804 complained of the unfair neglect of the opera, adding that, whereas the 'imposing', 'convulsive' strokes of *Don Giovanni* found a ready audience, the 'soft half-tints of the more refined worldly relationships [der feinern Weltverhältnisse], th[e] sweet rapture' of *Così* were beyond the reach of even the most refined spectators.[44] He continues:

This opera seems to be considered as the least important of Mozart's theatrical works, and this pains me. To be sure the oversimplicity of its subject, the weak delineation of the characters on the part of the poet, the inverisimilitude of the situations, the feebleness of the dénouement and above all the pitiful translations have contributed much to this judgement. All the greater then were the difficulties with which the composer had to battle. We wish to investigate now how he overcame these.

First one is struck by how delicately this opera is scored; how Mozart refrained from the sort of overburdening [of accompaniments] for which he has otherwise been criticized; how appropriately he has used the wind instruments. Add to that the harmony of the whole. . . the grace in the individual paintings, with what tenderness every emotion is handled; the truth of expression! The plot does not suffer any strong coloration, and yet such refined nuancing of the characters![45]

This entire passage was later plagiarized by Nissen, in his *Anhang zu W. A. Mozarts Biographie*.

An exceptional, completely enthusiastic assessment of the opera during this period comes from the arch-Romantic E. T. A. Hoffmann. In 'The poet and the composer', Hoffmann (who was both) has one of his interlocutors ask the other, with regard to opera buffa:

Ferdinand. But can music be expected to express comedy in all its nuances?
Ludwig. I am absolutely convinced it can, and artists of genius have proved it a hundred times. Music can convey, for example, an impression of

the most delicious irony, such as that pervading Mozart's splendid opera *Così fan tutte*.

Ferdinand. The thought now strikes me that, according to your principle, the despised libretto of that opera is in fact truly operatic.

Ludwig. And that's precisely what I meant when I said earlier that Mozart had chosen for his classical operas only librettos that exactly suited opera, although *Le nozze di Figaro* is more a play with songs than a true opera.[46]

As we shall see, Wagner's opinion of these two operas was precisely the opposite.

The opinion of Beethoven has weighed heavily against *Così fan tutte*. When asked in 1825 what genre of opera he might prefer to write, the composer is supposed to have told Ludwig Rellstab 'I could not write operas like *Don Juan* and *Così fan tutte*. I have an aversion to such things, for I find them too frivolous.'[47] In fact, the second opera in question was not *Così fan tutte*, but *Le nozze di Figaro*. (This passage from Rellstab's posthumously published memoirs has been repeatedly misquoted in the literature on the opera.)[48] The strongly moralistic Beethoven probably did hold such an opinion of *Così fan tutte*, but his imitation of the wayward Fiordiligi's *rondò*, and of the canon of the second finale, in his opera *Fidelio*, nevertheless shows that he knew the opera well. Without a trace of irony, Beethoven gives his heroine Leonore an aria ('Komm, Hoffnung') in the same E major and the same form as Fiordiligi's, with even more spectacular obbligato writing for not two horns, but three. In the opening scene of *Fidelio*, Beethoven uses a canonic quartet in much the same way as had Mozart in *Così*, as the characters simultaneously express their conflicting feelings of rapture and anxiety.

Even at a time when the opera was rarely performed in Italian, the public was still occasionally able to encounter *Così* without the camouflage of an altered text or setting. One reads, for instance, of concert performances of excerpts from the opera – as of the overture and second finale, in Frankfurt on Easter Sunday (!) 1804.[49] Engraved keyboard scores offered relatively original and (apart from the simple recitatives) complete versions of the work. The first was published in 1795 by Breitkopf, with others following in 1796 (Schott) and 1799 (Simrock); all included Bretzner's text in addition to Da Ponte's. No full score of *Così* was published until the Breitkopf and Härtel edition of 1810, but even before the turn of the century there was a flood of published arrangements for *Hausmusik* (e.g. keyboard, pairs of flutes, violin and piano, or string quartet), either of the complete opera, or of excerpts.[50]

During the Biedermeyer period, adaptations for the stage strayed ever farther from Da Ponte's text – though not without protests. A witness to a Prague performance of *Die Zauberprobe* (The magic trial), by the Viennese theatre-poet Treitschke (1814), praised Treitschke's intentions, but lamented that

where formerly we ran up against a shocking improbability, now we are offended by a magic spell which in a much coarser way lacks all poetic truth.[51]

Carl Alexander Herklots reworked the opera in verse as *Die verfängliche Wette* (The insidious bet; Berlin, 1820), in which not two but four suitors competed for the sisters, and a second servant, Pedrillo (!), took over Despina's functions in the finales. The addition of a new vocal part for this character was soundly criticized in an 1825 review as a 'falsification'.[52] London first saw Mozart's opera in 1811, at the King's Theatre, in Italian, but the Covent Garden production ten years later of *Tit for tat, or The tables turned*, 'altered and adapted from the *COSÌ FAN TUTTE*' gained rather greater currency. Of particular interest is J. D. Anton's *Die Guerillas*. (1837, for Frankfurt), whose text was no translation, but rather a 'new plot to [Mozart's] opera *Così fan tutte*', set now in a Spanish castle surrounded by bandits. Though Anton himself made no such claim, a reviewer of this production assumed that he had answered the call given out by Nissen (plagiarized from an 1801 article by Rochlitz, quoted above) to some German poet, to put together 'something different', drawing 'far more on the music than on the Italian text'.[53] The characters in this drama were motivated not by mere feelings of jealousy, pride or flirtatiousness, but rather by 'more important motives, such as patriotism, national pride and hatred, avarice, etc., and Mozart's music is no longer based on a vague foundation.'

The later nineteenth century

While bastardized versions of *Così* continued to be concocted (e.g. *Peines d'amour perdues*, after Shakespeare's *Love's labour lost*, by Jules Barbier and Michel Carré; Paris, 1863), around the middle of the century an opposite trend towards *Werktreue* began to assert itself, inspired in part, as Klaus Hortschansky has noted, by the first centenary of Mozart's birth.[54] Bernhard Gugler's 1856 version for Stuttgart, though still altering the plot and the order of the musical numbers, at least retained Mozart's score uncut. Eduard Devrient's influential 1860 version for Karlsruhe was the first in German to include all the recitatives – though he had few qualms about altering basic elements of the opera's plot (as in having Despina inform the women of the ruse at the beginning of Act II). The efforts of mid-century scholars such as Otto Jahn to rehabilitate the reputation of Da Ponte initially had little impact on the way the text was presented (as opposed to the music), but it was not long before they bore fruit.

Though performances of Così still lagged well behind those of Figaro and Don Giovanni,[55] the opera had by the 1850s reached the stages of most European opera houses. But with the rise of the Wagnerian aesthetic of opera, new obstacles to public understanding of Così were raised. The composer's polemic against 'number operas' made allowances for some products of Mozart's pen, but not for a work whose second act featured five consecutive arias, unrelieved by any ensembles. Wagner's operas, which eschewed such basic operatic conventions as end-rhyme, word-repetition and simultaneous speech, made many spectators view Mozart's works – and especially Così fan tutte – in a new, unflattering light. The new musical demands of Wagnerian music dramas threatened to drive Mozart's operas, if not into extinction, then at least decline and further distortion. 'It would now seem to be necessary to support a troupe of Mozart singers alongside the Wagner singers, indeed, even a separate Mozart orchestra alongside the Wagner orchestra', lamented one critic.[56] But it was the moral substance of the opera which most outraged Wagner and the Wagnerians. 'O, how doubly dear and above honour is Mozart to me,' wrote Wagner in Opera and drama, 'that it was not possible for him to invent music for Tito like that of Don Giovanni, for Cosi [sic] fan tutte like that to Figaro! How shamefully would it have desecrated Music!'[57] The like-minded Eduard Hanslick condemned the opera in 1875, declaring that 'the boundless triviality of the libretto everywhere deals a deathblow to Mozart's lovely music to Così fan tutte. The civilisation of our time cannot come to terms with it even with the best of intentions. . .I deem Così fan tutte to be no longer stageworthy.'[58] A production directed by Mahler at the Viennese Hofoper a quarter-century later did not substantially change his mind.

The twentieth century: rehabilitation

For Così fan tutte the twentieth century began in 1897, with an important new production in the Munich Residenztheater (site of the

1781 première of *Idomeneo*), conducted by Richard Strauss. The performances featured a new, basically faithful translation by Hermann Levi, and a rotating stage which allowed for quick changes of scene without the intervention of a curtain. There had been stirrings already of a movement towards reinstating the opera's original text, but until this Munich revival appreciation of the psychological subtleties of the libretto had been sorely lacking. It is no coincidence that this path-breaking production came during a period of great public interest in the investigations of Freud and others into the unconscious motivations – particularly sexual – of human behaviour. A Munich critic at the time described Mozart's opera as 'a high-spirited, lively play which, to be sure, seeks its effect only in interior, psychologically captivating incidents and not in death and slaughter', adding that 'music can only be dramatically conceived and experienced when it is heard with the situations and incidents for which it was written.'[59] Strauss, too, in a slightly later essay, emphasized the piece's psychological insights, also insisting on the necessity of judging the opera against the standards of its own era. Attacking the Wagnerian tradition to which he himself had once adhered, Strauss wrote (sarcastically, at first):

[I]n the magnificent scene of the Commendatore in *Don Giovanni* one felt in one's nerves something of what was considered dramatic in the good old days, and of what every good drama had to offer in the same or even greater intensity, if it were not to be cursed for not being dramatic. . .Today a community – still small, to be sure – takes pleasure from the charms of a more intimate, psychological, consistently developed and carefully shaded plot, without great to-do [ohne große Haupt- und Staatsaktionen], from the artistic treatment of a quite specific terrain of expression, such as that humoristic-pathetic, parodistic-sentimental style which is treated with such delicate irony in *Così fan tutte*. . .[60]

Despite the breakthrough of Munich, *Così* continued to be performed in all manner of fashions. In 1909 Dresden saw *Die Dame Kobold* (The lady goblin), a story after Calderón grafted onto Mozart's music by the Wagnerian baritone Carl Scheidemantel. *Così* was also subjected to rococo trivialization, encouraged in part by the *régisseur* Ernst Lert's heavy emphasis on its symmetry in his influential book *Mozart auf dem Theater* of 1918. Director Lothar Wallerstein and scenic designer Ludwig Sievert thrust the opera into the avant-garde with their 1928 Frankfurt production, in which stylization of both gesture and sets (which included a see-saw for the sisters) accentuated the artifice of the plot. And Strauss notwithstanding, *Così* was still often shorn of much of its music. The

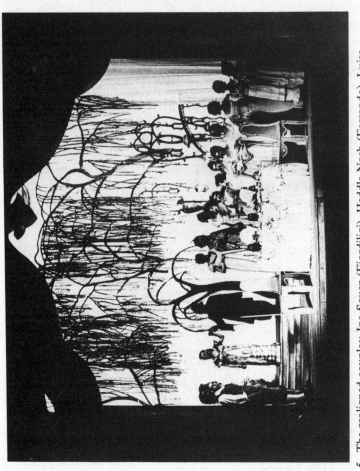

5 The realigned couples: Ina Souez (Fiordiligi), Heddle Nash (Ferrando), Luise Helletsgruber (Dorabella), and Willi Domgraf-Fassbaender (Guglielmo) are serenaded by the chorus in the 1934 production at Glyndebourne, conducted by Fritz Busch.

popular Dover score of the opera perpetuates to this day the 'usual' cuts recommended in Schünemann and Soldan's 1941 edition, which it reproduces.

Stimulus from England in the early part of this century was crucial in helping bring *Così fan tutte* back into the Mozart canon. In his pioneering book *Mozart's operas: A critical study* of 1913 (second edition 1947), Edward J. Dent wrote dismissively of the many retextings of the opera, saying

> There is not the least necessity for such a proceeding. *Così fan Tutte* is the best of all Da Ponte's librettos and the most exquisite work of art among Mozart's operas. It is as perfect a libretto as any composer could desire, though no composer but Mozart could ever do it justice. . .To appreciate the delicate filigree of Da Ponte's comedy, one must read every word of the Italian original and sing it through, recitatives and all, to Mozart's music.[61]

Dent himself helped revise M. E. Browne's translation for a 1926 Bristol production, but *Così* was not given again in England in Italian until 1934, when it was paired with *Le nozze di Figaro* for the inaugural season at Glyndebourne. *Così* made a profound impression on the public there (and on such influential critics as Tovey) – in part because of the small size of the auditorium, which fostered an intimacy of ensemble well suited to the work. The classic 1935 recording of the opera under director Fritz Busch was the first to present more than excerpts, though still not the entire work. (For that one had to wait until the 1967 recording under Erich Leinsdorf.)[62] *Così* was offered yearly at Glyndebourne through 1939, and almost as regularly after the war. These post-war productions, conducted by Vittorio Gui and Sir John Pritchard, were memorable for their high standards generally, and for individual performances such as that of Richard Lewis, for whom Ferrando's second-act arias posed few obstacles, and of Sena Jurinac as a complex and vulnerable Fiordiligi.[63]

In more recent decades, other singers of international renown have become identified with roles in *Così fan tutte* – none more than Elisabeth Schwarzkopf as Fiordiligi, whose repeated notes in the opening phrases of 'Come scoglio', sung as if through clenched teeth, are memorable as an indication of steadfastness. But modern directors have left rather more of an imprint on *Così* than singers, no doubt because the experiment of the opera's premise seemed to encourage experimentation as regards staging. Several principal trends can be identified, among them that of using stage design and movement to accentuate the symmetries of plot. For the Deutsche

Oper production of 1955, for instance, Jean-Pierre Ponnelle framed the entire stage in a symmetrical *rocaille* ornament, while Carl Ebert choreographed the farewell and wedding-banquet scenes in strict symmetry as well. Three self-standing doors in the 'room' of the second finale recalled the portals of Sarastro's realm, thus reminding one of the thematic connections between *Così* and *Die Zauberflöte*. Ponnelle revamped his production in 1969 and several times subsequently, opting for a less austere style, but still relying heavily on symmetrical framing devices.[64]

Ponnelle and many other directors have supplemented the sparse stage directions of *Così*'s eighteenth-century libretto with extra characters or stage business, so as to bring out various aspects of the work they deemed important – and to project the drama to auditoriums far larger than any envisioned by Da Ponte and Mozart. Götz Friedrich, in a 1975 Hamburg production, emphasized the sense of play by repeatedly bringing on a Neapolitan *commedia dell'arte* troupe; more recently, Sir Peter Hall has used the opera to explore the liberating effects of disguise and masks on the lovers themselves. Premature or accidental switching of the lovers early on in the Albanians' courtship has become a routine joke. Directorial intervention has also extended to fundamental changes in the dénouement. In 1955 Ebert and Ponnelle allowed only a grudging, imperfect reconciliation – playing against the music of the final pages of the opera, as it were.[65] Ferrando and Fiordiligi furtively sought each others' hands as the curtain descended on András Fricsay's 1974 Frankfurt production, and at the end of John Eliot Gardiner's 1992 staging at Lisbon, Ferrara and Paris, 'the original pairings are restored but it is clear that they won't last – Ferrando and Fiordiligi have found each other. Dorabella and Guglielmo are lost'.[66]

After more than a century of productions in which *Così fan tutte* was treated as little more than a farce, it is not surprising to find some modern directors and critics approaching the opera with deadly seriousness, as if to counteract this legacy. The philosopher Bernard Williams has specifically addressed the issue of the opera's proper tone:

To take *Così fan tutte* seriously is not, as people sometimes impatiently insist, to refuse to treat it as a comedy. On the contrary, it is to take it seriously as a comedy, something we are certainly prepared to do with other comedies, and with Mozart's other great Italian operas. Since one is dealing with an opera, that involves attending at once to the music and to the meaning of the action, and when one does that a problem certainly arises.[67]

The problem is not, as Wagner thought, that the music was adversely affected by the triviality of the plot, or that the musical seductions are not in earnest, but rather that the depths of feeling Mozart creates in the second act – particularly in response to the predicament of Fiordiligi – seem to be obliterated by the sudden reconciliation of the end.

Nothing is denied of what has happened; that is what is sad in this comedy, that all that dimension of feeling exists, but the world will rumble on as though it did not. Perhaps it may even be hinted that it is better that the world and its arrangements turn their back on that kind and depth of feeling.[68]

According to Williams, the ending thus lies open to various interpretations, irresolution prominent among them. This was the attitude taken by Johannes Schaaf in his production for Covent Garden and the Vienna Staatsoper in 1989: at the end of the drama the men pay off their lost debt, while their fiancées stand off to the side in a state of shock.[69] Conductor Nikolaus Harnoncourt seconded Schaaf's harsher vision not just here, but also in many ostensibly comic moments earlier in the opera. Jonathan Miller has likewise projected the seriousness inherent in the ending far back into the work, foregoing the usual antics of the Mesmerian cure in order to emphasize the pivotal aspect of renewal and rebirth that the process represents to the characters.[70]

In line with a general trend in opera productions, in recent years *Così* has been relocated and updated more often than not. The most thoroughgoing attempt at an updating recently has been that of Peter Sellars – actually a series of updatings, since the topical references have changed from one venue to the next. Sellars himself has described his approach as providing a 'visual counterpoint' to the music – which must be understood to include his translation of the text and printed commentary, as well as the staging.[71] Set in an American seaside diner (owned by Alfonso, with Despina as the waitress), Sellars's *Così* is relentlessly topical. (The sisters contemplate not portraits, but men's fashion magazines; the soldiers' disguises, which the women see through immediately, are borrowed from characters on an American television comedy.) This emphasis on allusiveness makes for something of the same type of experience that Da Ponte, with his many literary citations, had created for the opera's first audience. Even Sellars's substitution of a different aria for 'È Amore un ladroncello' is topical, in that Mozart had written the piece ('Vado, ma dove') for Louise Villeneuve, the first

6 Despina's diner: Sanford Sylvan (Alfonso), James Maddalena (Guglielmo), Janice Felty (Dorabella), Frank Kelley (Ferrando), and Susan Larson (Fiordiligi) in Peter Sellars's 1989 production of the opera, designed by Adrianne Lobel, at PepsiCo Summerfare, State University of New York, Purchase.

7   Maria Höglind (Dorabella), Lars Tibell (Ferrando), Ulla Severin (Despina), Enzo Florimo (Alfonso), Magnus Lindén (Guglielmo), and Ann Christine Biel (Fiordiligi), in Willy Decker's production at the Drottningholm Court Theatre, 1985.

8 Amanda Roocroft (Fiordiligi) and Rosa Mannion (Dorabella), in the 1992 production by John Eliot Gardiner, designed by Carlo Tommasi (Ferrara, Lisbon, Paris).

Dorabella, to sing in another opera. But the insertion of this anguished piece effectively turns Dorabella into another Fiordiligi, and removes the reference to the opera's title contained in the last line of the original aria. Sellars's dark vision of sexual relations is evident also in the second finale, in his deliberate mistranslation of the men's renunciation of further proofs, so as to preclude a reconciliation.

Sellars's is by no means the only avant-garde staging of *Così fan tutte*, thoughtful or thoughtless, in recent times. But an opposite trend towards 'authenticity' in such factors as musical forces, performing techniques and theatrical resources is also discernible. Though performances at the eighteenth-century theatre at Drottningholm (outside Stockholm) have thus far made little use of period gesture, the 1984 recording of *Così* by that theatre's original-instrument orchestra, conducted by Arnold Östman, was for many Mozartians a stunning revelation in terms of textures, pacing and hitherto unnoticed details of word-painting. Even 'mainstream' productions have increasingly featured singers younger than those one generally heard in the past, thereby 'creating a bridge to the eighteenth century' – a time when a Despina could sing of 'a woman of fifteen years', as Herbert Zeman has noted.[72] In all the efforts thus far towards a more eighteenth-century approach to performing Mozart's operas there has been an implicit confidence that close attention to the details of articulation, sonority, tempo and balance would bring with it additional insights into the characters and their motivations. Our degree of familiarity with eighteenth-century culture in general is no less important in this respect. But no amount of ancillary investigation will afford us anything approaching the profusion of insights into Mozart's century, and the human heart, that one reaps from spending time with the work itself. Like a great painting, *Così fan tutte* fascinates and teaches in direct proportion to its complexity, ambiguity and timelessness.

Notes

1 Introduction

1 *Mozart: Briefe und Aufzeichnungen*, ed. Wilhelm A. Bauer, Otto Erich Deutsch and Joseph Heinz Eibl, 7 vols. (Kassel, 1962–75), 4:99–100. All translations from Mozart's letters are my own.

2 Quoted in Otto Erich Deutsch, ed., *Mozart: Die Dokumente seines Lebens* (Kassel, 1961), p. 346.

3 Franz Xaver Němetschek (Niemetschek), *Lebensbeschreibung des k. k. Kapellmeisters Wolfgang Amadeus Mozart, aus Originalquellen* (Prague, 2/1808; repr. Leipzig, 1978), p. 43.

4 Aleksandr Ulybyshev, *Nouvelle biographie de Mozart, suivie. . .de l'analyse des principales œuvres de Mozart*, 3 vols. (Moscow, 1843), 3:307.

5 See Daniel Heartz, Chapter 13 ('Three schools for lovers, or "Così fan tutte le belle"'), in *Mozart's operas*, ed., with contributing essays, by Thomas Bauman (Berkeley and Los Angeles, 1990), pp. 217–27 (218); Andrew Steptoe, *The Mozart-Da Ponte operas: The cultural and musical background to Le nozze di Figaro, Don Giovanni, and Così fan tutte* (Oxford, 1988), pp. 132–4.

6 Edward J. Dent, *Mozart's operas: A critical study* (London, Oxford, New York, 2/1947), pp. 190, 206.

7 Ernst Gombrich, 'Così fan tutte (Procris included)', *Journal of the Warburg and Courtauld Institutes*, 17 (1954), 372–4.

8 Da Ponte, *Memorie*, ed. Cesare Pagnini (Milan, 1960), p. 135.

9 Unpublished paper by Elizabeth Dunstan, 'Da Ponte and Ariosto'. Though Alan Tyson has suggested that it was a last-minute suggestion of Mozart's to call the opera *Così fan tutte*, the phrase nevertheless stems from Da Ponte's pen, and was the title by which the opera was best known; see Tyson, *Mozart: Studies of the autograph scores* (Cambridge, Mass. and London, 1987), p. 197.

10 Heartz, *Mozart's operas*, p. 220.

11 See Gustav Gugitz, 'Das Annafest im alten Wien', in idem and Emil Karl Blümml, *Von Leuten und Zeiten im alten Wien* (Vienna and Leipzig, 1922), pp. 63–86 (66–7).

12 Nearly all of these references were retained in Paisiello's opera; indeed, the subtitle is the last line sung in the entire work.

13 Friedrich Rochlitz, 'Noch einige Kleinigkeiten aus Mozarts Leben', *Allgemeine musikalische Zeitung* 3:35 (27 May 1801), col. 590–6 (593).

2 Genesis

1 Da Ponte, *Memorie*, p. 135. All translations are mine unless otherwise noted.

2 Thorwart signed the marriage contract between Mozart and Constanze Weber as the latter's guardian. On Thorwart's influence on the operations of the Burgtheater, see Mozart's letter of 16 January 1782, in *Mozart: Briefe*, 3:191–2.

3 *An extract from the life of Lorenzo da Ponte, with the history of several dramas written by him, and among others, Il Figaro, Il Don Giovanni, & La scola degli amanti: set to music by Mozart* (New York, 1819), pp. 19–20.

4 Němetschek, *Lebensbeschreibung*, p. 43.

5 Georg Nikolaus von Nissen, *Anhang zu W. A. Mozarts Biographie, nach Originalbriefen, Sammlungen alles über ihn Geschriebenen, mit vielen neuen Beylagen, Steindrücken, Musikblättern und einem Facsimile*, ed. Constanze Mozart Nissen (Leipzig, 1828; repr. Hildesheim, 1964), pp. 92–3.

6 Friedrich Heinse, *Reise- und Lebens-Skizzen nebst dramaturgischen Blättern. 1. Teil* (Leipzig, 1837), p. 183 ff., quoted in Kurt Kramer, 'Da Pontes "Così fan tutte"', *Nachrichten der Akademie der Wissenschaften in Göttingen*, 1. Philologisch-historische Klasse, Jhrg. 1973, no. 1 (Göttingen, 1973), 1–27 (4).

7 Heinse's story of an imperial commission formed the premise of a Mozart-novel: *Così fan tutte: Mozarts Faschingsoper* by Hans Rudolf Bartsch (1912); see Hans-Peter Glöckner, 'Die Popularisierung der Unmoral: *Così fan tutte* in der Belletristik', in Vill, ed., *Beiträge*, 112–26 (114–5).

8 *A Mozart pilgrimage. Being the travel diaries of Vincent & Mary Novello in the year 1829*, ed. Rosemary Hughes (London, 1955), p. 127. The first comment was recorded by Mary Novello, the second by Vincent.

9 A-Wn, Musiksammlung, Suppl. Mus. 4531. Prof. Rice brought the score to my attention during July 1994 after finding it listed in the card catalogue; we then examined it jointly. Salieri's settings of these texts from *Così* have been mentioned neither in studies of his own works, nor in the Mozart literature.

10 Da Ponte, *Memorie*, p. 91.

11 Ibid., p. 136; and Vienna, Staatsarchiv, Vertrauliche Akten, Karton 40, Nr. 2 ('Cose dell' Ab. da Ponte'), fol. 19.

12 *Mozart: Briefe*, 3:268.

13 In the version for Salieri, this text is as follows:

> Terminiamo una volta
> Amici queste ciarle,
> Che ognun di voi la fedeltade vanti
> Della sua cara amata,
> Trovo naturalissimo: ma per me
> Rimarrò sempre nel dire ostantissimo:

(Once and for all, friends, let's stop this arguing; I find it very natural that each of you boasts of the fidelity of his dear beloved; as for me, I'll always remain obstinate in saying:)

14 Kramer, 'Da Pontes "Così fan tutte"', pp. 6–8.
15 Ibid., p. 16.
16 See János Fekete de Galántha, *Wien im Jahre 1787: Skizze eines lebenden Bildes von Wien, entworfen von einem Weltbürger*, transl. from the French and ed. Victor Klarwill (Vienna, 1921), p. 12.
17 Da Ponte, *Memorie*, p. 136.
18 See Jonathan Miller, *Subsequent performances* (New York, 1986), p. 200.
19 See the letter of 23 January 1778 from Joseph Mesmer to Leopold Mozart, quoted in Deutsch, *Dokumente*, p. 154.
20 Robert Darnton, *Mesmerism and the end of the Enlightenment in France* (Cambridge, Mass., 1968), pp. 8–9.
21 Already in 1776 Mozart had set a buffo aria text with Mesmerian overtones: 'Clarice cara', K256, which begins with the lines:

    Clarice cara
    mia sposa dev'essere
    per la magnetica
    virtù simpatica. . .

22 Darnton, *Mesmerism*, p. 10.
23 H. C. Robbins Landon, *Mozart: The golden years* (London and New York, 1989), p. 62.
24 Johann Pezzl, *Skizze von Wien [1786–1790]. Ein Kultur- und Sittenbild aus der josefinischen Zeit*, ed. Gustav Gugitz and Anton Schlossar (Graz, 1923), p. 435. A large selection of passages was translated by H. C. Robbins Landon in *Mozart and Vienna* (London and New York, 1991).
25 Joachim Perinet, *29 Ärgernisse* (Vienna, 1786), cited in Otto Schindler, 'Das Publikum des Burgtheaters in der Josephinischen Ära', in Margaret Dietrich, ed., *Das Burgtheater und sein Publikum*, 1 (Vienna, 1976), pp. 11–95 (48).
26 Naples was apparently not the setting in Da Ponte's initial conception of *Così*, for in Mozart's autograph score, Fiordiligi's lines 'Da Napoli partiti / Sono gli amanti nostri' originally read 'Da Trieste partiti. . .'.
27 Dunstan, 'Da Ponte and Ariosto', pp. 7–8.
28 See Heartz, *Mozart's operas*, p. 252. 'Mongibello' was used by Da Ponte also as a character's name, in the 1830 version for New York of his pasticcio *L'ape musicale* (The musical bee). That work too opens in a caffè.
29 Tyson's findings are summarized below without further citation from Chapter 13, 'On the composition of Mozart's *Così fan tutte*', in *Mozart: Studies of the autograph scores* (Cambridge, Mass. and London, 1987), pp. 177–221; this account is a slightly revised version of his article 'Notes on the composition of Mozart's *Così fan tutte*', *Journal of the American Musicological Society*, 37:2 (Summer 1984), 356–401.
30 Tyson, 'On the composition of Mozart's *Così fan tutte*', p. 183.
31 See Tyson, *Mozart: Studies of the autograph scores*, p. 194.
32 See Heartz, *Mozart's operas*, pp. 244–6.
33 Letter to Puchberg, late December 1789; *Mozart: Briefe*, 4:100.
34 Friedrich Rochlitz, '*Nachschrift* zur Recension von Eyblers Requiem', in *Allgemeine musikalische Zeitung*, 28:21 (24 May 1826), col. 337–40 (338).
35 See Rudolph Angermüller, 'Weigl, Joseph (ii)', in *New Grove*, 20:296–8 (296).

36 Dexter Edge, 'Mozart's fee for *Così fan tutte*', in *Journal of the Royal Musical Association*, 116:2 (November 1991), 211–35.

3 Synopsis

1 Ulybyshev, *Nouvelle biographie de Mozart*, 3:327.
2 'Sei tu pazzo? Vuoi tu precipitarti / Per una donna che non vale [un caz**]'; see Noiray, 'Commentaire musical et littéraire', *L'avant-scène Opéra: Così fan tutte*, No. 131–2 (May–June 1990), 39–144 (116).
3 The arias in question are Semiramide's 'Tradita, sprezzata' in the opera of that title, and Megacle's 'Se cerca, se dice' in *L'Olimpiade*; see Reinhard Strohm, *Italienische Opernarien des frühen Settecento (1720–1730)* (*Analecta musicologica*, 16:1–2; Cologne, 1976), 1:63–5.
4 Dent, *Mozart's operas*, p. 206.

4 The sources of an 'original' libretto

1 Da Ponte, *Memorie*, pp. 106 and 118.
2 Anon., *Anti-da Ponte. . .* (Vienna, 1791), p. 15.
3 Ibid., pp. 59 and 62.
4 See Daniela Goldin, *La vera fenice: Librettisti e libretti tra Sette e Ottocento* (Turin, 1985), pp. 27 ff.
5 See the already cited works of Gombrich and Kramer, and Andrew Steptoe, 'The sources of *Così fan tutte*: A reappraisal', *Music and letters*, 62 (1981), 281–94, incorporated within Chapter 6 of *The Mozart–Da Ponte operas: The cultural and musical background to Le nozze di Figaro, Don Giovanni, and Così fan tutte* (Oxford, 1988).
6 Quotations are from the translation by Frank Justus Miller, in Ovid, *Metamorphoses*, vol. 1, 3d edn. revised by G. P. Goold (Cambridge, Mass. and London, 1984).
7 Steptoe, *The Mozart–Da Ponte operas*, p. 125.
8 Tim Carter, 'Ariosto, Ludovico' and 'Tasso, Torquato', in *The New Grove dictionary of opera*, ed. Stanley Sadie, 4 vols. (London, 1992), 1:191–2 and 4:656–7, respectively.
9 This and a number of other parallels between *Così fan tutte* and Canto 43 of Ariosto's poem were first noted by Kurt Kramer, in 'Da Pontes "Così fan tutte",' p. 13 ff. English versions throughout this book of passages from Ariosto's poem are from the translation by John Hoole (5 vols.; London, 1773).
10 See Dent, *Mozart's operas*, p. 110, n. 1, and Carter, *W. A. Mozart: Le nozze di Figaro*, p. 155, n. 6.
11 Da Ponte, *Memorie*, pp. 14–15.
12 Dunstan, 'Da Ponte and Ariosto', pp. 9, 4.
13 Ibid., pp. 24 ff.
14 Ibid., pp. 3–4.
15 The tale was later taken up by La Fontaine (*Joconde, ou l'Infidélité des femmes*) and other writers, even librettists.
16 Steptoe, *The Mozart–Da Ponte operas*, pp. 126–7.
17 Dunstan, 'Da Ponte and Ariosto', p. 8.

18 Despina's name reproduces the pronunciation of the modern Greek word 'despoina', which means 'mistress', though this does not exclude an Ariostan origin. I am grateful to Michel Noiray for this information.
19 Dunstan, 'Da Ponte and Ariosto', p. 23.
20 Ibid., p. 18. This image goes back ultimately to Virgil's *Æeid*; see Heartz, *Mozart's operas*, p. 249.
21 Dunstan, 'Da Ponte and Ariosto', p. 19 ff.
22 Ibid., pp. 13–14. See also Wolfgang Osthoff, 'Gli endecasillabi villotistici in *Don Giovanni* e *Nozze di Figaro*', *Venezia e il melodramma nel Settecento*, ed. Maria Teresa Muraro (Florence, 1981), 2:293–311 (293–4).
23 Da Ponte, *Memorie*, p. 128.
24 Heartz, *Mozart's operas*, p. 218.
25 Charles Rosen, *The classical style* (New York, 1971), p. 314.
26 Steptoe, *The Mozart–Da Ponte operas*, p. 133.
27 Nicholas Till, *Mozart and the Enlightenment: Truth, virtue and beauty in Mozart's operas* (London and Boston, 1991), pp. 235–6. I am grateful to Daniel Heartz for bringing Till's book, then still unpublished, to my attention.
28 See Viktor Golubev, *Marivaux' Lustspiele in deutschen Übersetzungen des 18. Jahrhunderts* (Heidelberg, 1904), p. 105 ff.
29 See Frank H. Ellis, *Sentimental comedy: Theory and practice* (Cambridge, 1991), Chapter 1.
30 Ibid., p. 39.
31 I am grateful to John Rice for this information, from his forthcoming study of Gassmann's protégé Salieri. The letter in which Joseph discusses the opera, preserved in the Vienna Staatsarchiv, is dated 7 September 1771.
32 Heartz, *Mozart's operas*, pp. 230–2.
33 A 'ladies-fop, a dangler about women' (Giuseppe Baretti, *Dizionario delle lingue italiana, ed inglese*, 2 vols. [Venice, 1787]); the reference is Despina's, in the opening scene of Act II.
34 Da Ponte, *Memorie*, p. 12.
35 I am grateful to Dr Dorothea Link for bringing these and other Viennese operatic canons to my attention; see her article 'The Viennese operatic canon and Mozart's *Così fan tutte*', *Mitteilungen der Internationalen Stiftung Mozarteum*, 38 (1990), 111–21.
36 See Michael Kelly, *Reminiscences of Michael Kelly, of the King's Theatre, and Theatre Royal Drury Lane, including a period of nearly half a century; with original anecdotes of many distinguished persons, political, literary, and musical*, 2 vols. (London, 1826), 1:153.
37 Heartz, *Mozart's operas*, p. 229.
38 Dorothea Link, personal communication, 17 April 1991.
39 See Dorothea Link, '"Così fan tutte": Dorabella and Amore', in *Mozart-Jahrbuch* 1991 (Bericht über den Internationalen Mozart-Kongreß Salzburg 1991; Kassel, 1992), 2:888–94 (891).
40 Da Ponte, *Memorie*, p. 99.
41 Ibid., p. 98.
42 See John A. Rice, '*Scuola de' gelosi, La*', in *The New Grove dictionary of opera*, ed. Stanley Sadie, 4 vols. (London, 1992), 4:278.

43 Cited by Alfred Einstein, in *Mozart: His character, his work*, transl.
    Arthur Mendel and Nathan Broder (Oxford, 1945), p. 444. The passage
    occurs in Ch. 43 of Part I; see *Mémoires de M. Goldoni, pour servir à
    l'histoire de sa vie, et à celle de son théâtre* (1787), ed. Giuseppe Ortolani,
    in Goldoni, *Tutte le opere* (Milan, 2/1943), 1:197.
44 Letter of 16 June 1781 to Leopold Mozart, in Wolfgang Mozart, *Briefe*,
    3:132.

5 Così fan tutte, or 'La Partie carrée': the eighteenth-century context of a theatrical subject

1 An excellent survey of this sort is provided by Kritsch and Zeman in
    their article 'Das Rätsel eines genialen Opernentwurfs', pp. 364–70.
2 Miller, *Subsequent performances*, pp. 199–200.
3 This side of Alfonso's personality is reinforced in Christoph Friedrich
    Bretzner's translation (for Leipzig, 1794) of the officers' comments on
    the foolishness of old poets such as him, following No. 2:
    >   Fer.: Sie sind ein Weiberfeind!
    >   Gugl.: Wie die alten Philosophen gewöhnlich!

    (*Fer.:* You are a mysogynist! *Gugl.:* Like the ancient philosophers
    generally!)
4 *Dictionnaire portatif de la langue françoise, extrait du grand dictionnaire
    de Pierre Richelet*, ed. de Wailly (Lyons, 1775).
5 Giacomo Casanova, *Mémoires*, ed. Robert Abirached and Elio Zorzi, 3
    vols. (Paris, 1958–60), 1:644.
6 Thomas Kavanagh, *Writing the truth: Authority and desire in Rousseau*
    (Berkeley, Los Angeles and London, 1987), p. 89.
7 Quoted in Till, *Mozart and the Enlightenment*, p. 253; the passage is
    given in its most extensive form in the *Supplément au voyage de
    Bougainville*, and paraphrased elsewhere.
8 See Till, *Mozart and the Enlightenment*, p. 246
9 See, for instance, Vadé's *Le Trompeur trompé* (Paris, 1754), and Chiari
    and Bertoni's *L'ingannatore ingannato* (Venice, 1764).
10 Pezzl, *Faustin oder Das aufgeklärte philosophische Jahrhundert* (n.p.,
    1783); see Deutsch, *Dokumente*, p. 509.
11 Translated in H. C. Robbins Landon, *Mozart and Vienna* (London and
    New York, 1991), p. 128.
12 Pezzl, *Skizze*, p. 98 (this passage and some others below are not among
    Landon's excerpts).
13 Ibid., p. 96.
14 Quoted in Landon, *Mozart and Vienna*, pp. 111–12. In eighteenth-
    century Italy, such a lover was known as a *cicisbeo*; in German, the
    term *Hausfreund* sometimes had (and still has) this connotation
    (personal communication, Dexter Edge).
15 Pezzl, *Skizze*, p. 100.
16 See Rushton, *Don Giovanni*, p. 142.
17 Casanova, *Mémoires*, 1:1035.
18 Ibid., 1:922.
19 Ibid., 1:595.
20 Ibid., 1:445.

21 Ibid., 1:482–3.
22 Ibid., 1:653.
23 Ibid., 1:758.
24 Ibid., 1:947.
25 Quoted in the translation by P. W. K. Stone (London, 1961).
26 Ulybyshev, *Nouvelle Biographie*, p. 305.
27 See Till, *Mozart and the Enlightenment*, p. 255. Eduard had originally shared the name Otto with his childhood friend (the later Captain), but relinquished it in order to avoid confusion.
28 Johann Wolfgang von Goethe, *Die Wahlverwandtschaften*, in *Goethes sämtliche Werke*, 15 vols. (Leipzig, n.d.), 10:41.
29 Ibid., 10:83.
30 Ibid., 10:72.
31 *Theatralischer Guckkasten* (Vienna, 1807), p. 6; cited in Kritsch and Zeman, 'Das Rätsel eines genialen Opernentwurfs', p. 375.

6   The musical dramaturgy of the opera

1 Vincent and Mary Novello, *A Mozart pilgrimage*, p. 94.
2 See Goldoni's amusing summaries (in earlier and later versions) of the principles involved, with respect to serious opera, in Goldoni, *Tutte le opere*, 1:688–9 and 127–9.
3 See Ferguson and Rehm, eds., in Mozart, *Neue Ausgabe sämtlicher Werke*, II/5:xviii (Kassel, 1991), p. xxv.
4 See Margret Dietrich, 'Dokumentation zur Uraufführung', in *Così fan tutte: Beiträge zur Wirkungsgeschichte von Mozarts Oper* (Schriften zum Musiktheater, 2), ed. Susanne Vill (Bayreuth, 1978), 24–53 (43).
5 For a concise introduction to the principles of Italian versification, see Chapter 5, 'Verse and music in *Le nozze di Figaro*', in the Cambridge Opera Handbook for this opera by Tim Carter.
6 See Ignaz von Mosel, transl., *Ueber das Leben und die Werke des Anton Salieri, k. k. Hofkapellmeisters* (Vienna, 1827), pp. 30–2; quoted in Heartz, *Mozart's operas*, pp. 139, 154–5.
7 The range of opinion on the latter issue is defined on the one hand by Sigmund Levarie, *Mozart's Le nozze di Figaro* (Chicago, 1952), and on the other by James Webster, 'Mozart's operas and the myth of musical unity', *Cambridge opera journal*, 2 (1990), 197–218.
8 On Da Ponte's part in this, see Paolo Gallarati, 'Music and masks in Lorenzo Da Ponte's Mozartian librettos', *Cambridge opera journal*, 1:3 (November 1989), 225–47 (228).
9 Ulybyshev, *Nouvelle biographie de Mozart*, 3:307–8.
10 Kunze, *Mozarts Opern* (Stuttgart, 1984), p. 450.
11 Ibid., pp. 445–6.
12 On the ambiguities of this and other numbers in this opera, see also Mary Hunter, '*Così fan tutte* et les conventions musicales de son temps', *L'avant-scène Opéra: Così fan tutte*, no. 131–2 (May–June 1990), 158–64.
13 Kunze, *Mozarts Opern*, p. 497.
14 The translation is that of John Hoole, from *Dramas and other poems of the Abbé Pietro Metastasio*, 3 vols. (London, 1800), *Demetrius* (1:311–98).

15 Letter of 26 September 1781 to his father; see the discussion in Thomas Bauman, *W. A. Mozart: Die Entführung aus dem Serail* (Cambridge Opera Handbooks; Cambridge, 1987), pp. 85–8.

16 See also the mirror-image text and part-writing as the couples propose a toast in the second finale ('Tocca e bevi / Bevi e tocca', bb. 169–72).

17 Rochlitz, 'Noch einige Kleinigkeiten aus Mozarts Leben', *Allgemeine musikalische Zeitung* 3:35 (27 May 1801), col. 590–6 (593–4).

18 In this number the women prove to be quite accurate in their predictions of the sterotypical endearments the suitors will use. Additionally, Fiordiligi's exaggerated declamation at 'sospirando i sospiretti' (bb. 12–14) recalls the more heartfelt sighs of her sister's first aria, and anticipates Despina's sighs in her half of No. 22, as well as Fiordiligi and Ferrando's own 'sighs of delight' in No. 29 (bb. 120 ff.); see Heartz, *Mozart's operas*, p. 248.

19 Ibid., pp. 246–9.

20 I am grateful to Michel Noiray for this observation.

21 In addition to musical recalls within *Così*, there are of course numerous echoes of music from Mozart's earlier comedies. In many cases these would have resulted from the composer's similar, unconscious response to a similar situation — e.g. the falling scales, beginning with a syncopation, in the *stretti* of the sextet in *Don Giovanni* and the first finale of *Così*, in which fear is mixed with confusion (see Frits Noske, '*Così fan tutte*: Dramatic irony', in *The signifier and the signified: Studies in the operas of Mozart and Verdi* [The Hague, 1977], pp. 65–8). Elsewhere, as in Exx. 6.12a–d above, a more specific, conscious connection was intended.

22 Friedrich Rochlitz, 'Noch einige Kleinigkeiten aus Mozarts Leben', col. 591.

23 For an excellent survey of the sorts of operatic parody found in opera buffa of this period, see Mary Hunter, 'Some representations of *opera seria* in *opera buffa*', *Cambridge opera journal*, 3:2 (July 1991), 89–108.

24 Rochlitz, 'Noch einige Kleinigkeiten aus Mozarts Leben', col. 593.

25. Daniel Heartz notes the relationship between the breathless ostinato figure here and the turning figure which functions similarly in Elettra's aria; see Heartz, *Mozart's operas*, pp. 247–8.

26 E.g. by Andrew Steptoe, *The Mozart–Da Ponte operas*, p. 223.

27 Cf. Sonnet CLXV in Petrarch's *Canzoniere*.

28 My analysis draws upon that of James Webster, in 'The analysis of Mozart's arias', in Cliff Eisen, ed., *Mozart studies* (Oxford, 1991), pp. 101–99 (122–3).

29 See Noiray, 'Commentaire', p. 113.

30 Ibid., p. 115.

31 Rochlitz, 'Noch einige Kleinigkeiten aus Mozarts Leben', col. 593.

32 See Noske, 'Dramatic irony', pp. 93–120 (100).

33 See Da Ponte, *Memorie*, pp. 96–7.

34 See Noske, 'Dramatic irony', p. 101.

35 Stefan Kunze nevertheless saw this passage as completely 'serious'; see Kunze, *Mozarts Opern*, p. 450. Noske, on the other hand ('Dramatic irony', pp. 103–6), points to the ironic use of diminished melodic intervals here and generally in the opera.

36 See Platoff, 'Musical and dramatic structure in the *opera buffa* finale', *Journal of musicology*, 7 (1989), 191–230.
37 E.g. Hans Keller, in 'Mozart's wrong key signature', *Tempo*, 98 (1972), 21–7.
38 See Kunze, *Mozarts Opern*, p. 521.
39 See Noske, 'Dramatic irony', p. 115, from which our example is taken.
40 Ibid., p. 118.
41 Hermann Abert (*W. A. Mozart . . .*, 6th edn. (Leipzig, 1924), p. 652) also notes the 'trio-like' theme of bars 59–65, in the rhythm of the main theme of the *Figaro* overture.
42 So called by Dent in *Mozart's operas*, p. 193. Taking the uses of quotation as clues to the whole, Stefan Kunze ('Schein und Sein in Mozarts Ouvertüre zu «*Così fan tutte*»', *Schweizer Jahrbuch für Musikwissenschaft*, Neue Folge 3 (1983), 65–78 (68)) described the Presto as a sort of 'Musikalischer Spaß', as if the title might be altered to read 'Così fan tutt*i*. . .gli altri compositori di drammi buffi'. But Mozart is unlikely to have put professional rivalry above the more immediate task of preparing the minds of the spectators for the drama to come.
43 Donald Francis Tovey, 'The Overture to "Così fan tutte",' in *Essays in musical analysis* (Oxford, 1935–9), 6:30–1.
44 Ulybyshev, *Nouvelle Biographie de Mozart*, 3:327.

7   Performance and criticism

1   As in the 1782 Milanese première of Sarti's *Fra i due litiganti il terzo gode*.
2   See Michtner, Otto, *Das alte Burgtheater als Opernbühne von der Einführung des deutschen Singspiels (1778) bis zum Tod Kaiser Leopolds II. (1792)* (Theatergeschichte Österreichs, 3:1; Graz, Vienna, Cologne, 1970), pp. 150 and 158–9.
3   See Kelly, *Reminiscences*, 1:259.
4   See Patricia Lewy Gidwitz and John A. Rice, 'Ferrarese, Adriana', in *The New Grove dictionary of opera*, 2:162.
5   See John A. Rice, 'Rondò vocali di Salieri e Mozart per Adriana Ferrarese', in *I vicini di Mozart*, ed. Maria Teresa Muraro and David Bryant (Florence, 1989), 185–209 (188). Much of the following information on this singer is derived from Rice's article.
6   See Michtner, *Das alte Burgtheater*, pp. 272–3.
7   Letter of 26 July 1788, quoted in Rudolf Payer von Thurn, *Joseph II. als Theaterdirektor* (Vienna and Leipzig, 1920), p. 81.
8   *Grundsätze zur Theaterkritik, über Einsicht Sprache und Spiel in Menschenhaß und Reue* (Vienna, 1790), pp. 39–40.
9   Da Ponte, *Memorie*, p. 135.
10 Letter to Constanze Mozart of 19 (?) August 1789, in Mozart, *Briefe*, 4:97.
11 Example 7.3 is reproduced from Rice, 'Rondò vocali', p. 203.
12 See Da Ponte, *Memorie*, pp. 135 and 150.
13 Carl Ferdinand Pohl, *Joseph Haydn*, 2 vols. (Leipzig, 1878–82), 2:124.
14 *Grundsätze*, p. 41. The writer for the *Wiener Diarium* who described her début on 6 September 1789, as Cupid in *L'arbore di Diana*, was more

generous, praising 'her enchanting appearance, expressive acting and beautiful, artistic singing' (*Wiener Zeitung*, 1789, p. 1673; quoted in Michtner, Das alte Burgtheater, p. 286).

15 See Michtner, *Das alte Burgtheater*, p. 286.

16 Zinzendorf, entry for 11 February 1791, quoted in Michtner, op. cit., p. 425. On the length of Villeneuve's tenure, see Rice, 'Emperor and impresario: Leopold II and the transformation of Viennese musical theater, 1790–1792', Ph.D. thesis (Univ. of California, Berkeley, 1987), p. 53.

17 *Grundsätze*, p. 39.

18 Tyson, *Studies*, p. 138.

19 See Ferguson and Rehm's preface to their edition of the opera in the *Neue Mozart-Ausgabe*, II/5:xviii, p. xxv.

20 See Christopher Raeburn, 'Bussani, Francesco', in *The New Grove*, 3:512.

21 See Da Ponte's account of this episode in his *Memorie*, pp. 116–7.

22 Da Ponte, *Memorie*, p. 135. Later (p. 150), Da Ponte puts such words in the mouth of Emperor Leopold, the charges now including 'out-of-tune howling'.

23 *Grundsätze*, p. 40.

24 *Journal des Luxus und der Moden* (March 1790); quoted in Deutsch, *Dokumente*, pp. 318–19.

25 Quoted in Deutsch, *Dokumente*, p. 318.

26 Novello, *A Mozart pilgrimage*, p. 94.

27 Dexter Edge, 'Mozart's reception in Vienna, 1787–1791', in *Wolfgang Amadè Mozart: Essays on his life and his music* (Oxford University Press; in press).

28 See Rice, *W. A. Mozart: La clemenza di Tito* (Cambridge, 1991; Cambridge Opera Handbooks), pp. 8–9. See also the same author's 'Emperor and impresario', Chapters 2–3.

29 See Karin Werner-Jensen, '*Così fan tutte* im Angebot der Musik-verleger', in Vill, ed., *Beiträge*, pp. 99–111 (109).

30 Franz Xaver Němetschek, report on the Italian opera in Prague (December 1794), quoted in Rice, *W. A. Mozart: La clemenza di Tito*, p. 56.

31 *Allgemeine musikalische Zeitung*, 14:12 (18 March 1812), col. 189.

32 [Report from Dresden], *Allgemeine musikalische Zeitung*, 16:9 (2 March 1814), cols. 154–5.

33 Philip Gossett, program essay for the Saint Louis Opera, quoted in Andrew Porter, 'Musical events', *The New Yorker* (6 July 1992), 67–9 (69).

34 See Rudolf Angermüller, 'Bemerkungen zu französischen Bearbeitungen des 19. Jahrhunderts', in Vill, ed., *Beiträge*, 67–90.

35 See Gabriele Brandstetter, 'So machen's alle: Die frühen Übersetzungen von Da Pontes und Mozarts "Così fan tutte" für deutsche Bühnen', *Musikforschung*, 35:1 (January-March 1982), 27–44 (27).

36 See Manfred Schuler, 'Eine Prager Singspielfassung von Mozarts "Così fan tutte" aus der Zeit des Komponisten', *Mozart-Jahrbuch* 1991 (Bericht über den Internationalen Mozart-Kongreß Salzburg 1991; Kassel, 1992), 2:895–901.

37 This might be translated as 'The fidelity of women, or The girls are from Flanders' (whose inhabitants were proverbial for their fickleness in love). Bretzner was the author of the libretto which had served as the model for Stephanie and Mozart's *Die Entführung aus dem Serail*.

38 See Klaus Hortschansky, 'Gegen Unwahrscheinlichkeit und Frivolität: die Bearbeitung im 19. Jahrhundert', in Vill, ed., *Beiträge*, pp. 54–66 (57).

39 At the second Viennese revival in 1804, the 'Sansculots' had reverted to 'Armenier'. At the 1804 performances ten of the original 31 numbers were cut, including even 'Tutti accusan le donne'. The duet 'Fra gli amplessi' was replaced altogether; a quotation from this piece was substituted for Ferrando's self-introduction as a 'Cavaliere dell'Albania', in an attempt to repair this loose end in the second finale.

40 In his preface to the libretto, Bretzner had explained that 'This aria had to be encored in the [Italian-language] performances here [in Leipzig], whereby, to be sure, the poor ladies were a bit hard pressed. Should it be deemed offensive then if, in the event an encore is demanded, the actor gives men their due and sings the parody?'

41 Quoted from Schröder's diary by F. L. W. Meyer in *Fr. L. Schröder* (Hamburg, 1819), 2:1:63, cited in Deutsch, *Dokumente*, p. 346.

42 Quoted by Peter Ackermann, in 'Zwischen Kritik und Provokation: *Così fan tutte* in den Programmheften', in Vill, ed., *Beiträge*, pp. 175–82 (176). In this Weimar production some 11 numbers were eliminated; see Karl-Heinz Köhler, 'Die Rezeption der Mozart-Opern unter Goethes Theaterleitung im Jahrzehnt nach dem Tode des Komponisten: Ein Beitrag zur Wirkungsgeschichte des Mozartschen Schaffens im Spiegel der Weimarer Klassik', in *Mozart-Jahrbuch* 1991, 231–6 (235).

43 Rochlitz, 'Noch einige Kleinigkeiten aus Mozarts Leben', col. 592.

44 Anon., 'MISCELLEN. An meinem Freund', in *Allgemeine musikalische Zeitung*, 6:26 (28 March 1804), cols. 421–4 (422).

45 Ibid., cols. 422–4.

46 From 'The poet and the composer' (1813), translated by Martyn Clarke, in David Charlton, ed., *E. T. A. Hoffmann's musical writings: Kreisleriana, The poet and the composer, music criticism* (Cambridge, 1989), pp. 188–209 (203).

47 Quoted by Rudolph Angermüller, *Mozart's operas*, transl. Stewart Spencer (New York, 1988), p. 205; also by Peter Ackermann, in 'Zwischen Kritik und Provokation', p. 176; and by numerous other authors.

48 See Rellstab, *Aus meinem Leben*, 2 vols. (Berlin, 1861), 2:224 ff.

49 Among the singers on that occasion was Mozart's first love, Aloysia Weber Lange; see the *Allgemeine musikalische Zeitung*, 6:32 (9 May 1804), cols. 540–1.

50 See Werner-Jensen, '*Così fan tutte* im Angebot der Musikverleger', pp. 104–5.

51 Review in the *Allgemeine musikalische Zeitung*, 1823, quoted by Heinz Zietsch, 'Die Berichterstattung in den Musikzeitschriften und Tageszeitungen des 19. Jahrhunderts', in Vill, ed., *Beiträge*, 132–47 (134).

52 On both these versions, see Hortschansky, 'Gegen Unwahrscheinlichkeit und Frivolität', p. 57.

53 Review in the *Frankfurter Konversationsblatt* (15 December 1837), and Rochlitz, 'Noch einige Kleinigkeiten aus Mozarts Leben', col. 592; cited by Hortschansky, 'Gegen Unwahrscheinlichkeit und Frivolität', pp. 59–60.

54 Ibid., p. 54. Much of what follows is derived from Hortschansky's article.

55 See for instance Susanne Vill's 'Aufführungsstatistik 1790–1975', in Vill, ed., *Beiträge*, 283–7.

56 *Schwäbische Kronik*, 14 December 1891; quoted in Zietsch, 'Berichterstattung', p. 139.

57 Wagner, *Oper und Drama* (1851), in *Richard Wagner's prose works*, transl. William Ashton Ellis, 8 vols. (London, 1892–9; repr. New York, 1966), 2:37.

58 Hanslick, *Die moderne Oper: Kritiken und Studien* (Berlin, 1875), pp. 43–4; reprinted in Csampai and Holland, eds., *Così fan tutte: Texte, Materialien, Kommentare* (Hamburg, 1984), pp. 228–32 (229).

59 Oskar Merz, in *Münchener neueste Nachrichten*, 50:290 (27 June 1897); quoted in Zietsch, 'Berichterstattung', p. 142.

60 Strauss, 'Mozarts *Così fan tutte*' (1910); quoted in Csampai and Holland, eds., *Così fan tutte: Texte, Materialien, Kommentare*, pp. 233–9 (237–8).

61 Dent, *Mozart's operas*, p. 190.

62 See Alan Blyth and Malcolm Walker, *Opera on record* (London, 1979), '*Così fan tutte*', pp. 86–105 (96).

63 Ibid., pp. 88–9.

64 See Susanne Vill, 'Meinungen zum Thema: Die Inszenierungen von Carl Ebert 1955; Günther Rennert 1972; Jean-Pierre Ponnelle 1972; András Fricsay 1974', in Vill, ed., *Beiträge*, 190–212 (191–5, 199–203).

65 Vill, 'Meinungen', p. 194.

66 David Stevens, 'A Mozart jewel at Paris's Châtelet', *International herald tribune*, 8 July 1992.

67 Bernard Williams, 'Passion and cynicism: Remarks on *Così fan tutte*', *The musical times*, 114:1562 (April 1973), 361–4 (361).

68 Ibid., p. 364.

69 Manfred Blumauer, *Opernwelt*, 31:2 (February 1990), 33–4 (34).

70 Miller, *Subsequent performances*, p. 200.

71 See David Littlejohn, 'Reflections on Peter Sellars's Mozart', *Opera quarterly*, 7:2 (Summer 1990), 6–36 (20). Sellars's *Così* was first seen at Ipswich, Massachusetts, in 1984; it is better known from 1989 performances at the PepsiCo Summerfare at Purchase, New York, and from later television broadcasts.

72 See Herbert Zeman's comments in the discussion of Vill, 'Meinungen', p. 211.

Select bibliography

Primary sources

Anon., *Anti-da Ponte. I. Das von dem Abbate da Ponte vor seiner Abreise von Wien aufgestellte Denkmal des tiefsten Respekts gegen den Monarchen, und der gränzenlosen Achtung und Dankbarkeit gegen die österreichische Nation. Zergliedert und zur Beherzigung aufgedeckt von einem Cosmopoliten. II. Der vor dem Richterstuhle des Apollo angeklagte Theaterdichter des italienischen Singspieles; mit seiner Vertheidigung, und dem darauf erfolgten Endurtheile* (Vienna, 1791)

Grundsätze zur Theaterkritik, über Einsicht Sprache und Spiel in Menschenhaß und Reue (Vienna, 1790)

Casanova, Giacomo, *Mémoires*, ed. Robert Abirached and Elio Zorzi, 3 vols. (Paris, 1958–60)

Da Ponte, Lorenzo, *An extract from the life of Lorenzo da Ponte, with the history of several dramas written by him, and among others, Il Figaro, Il Don Giovanni, & La scola degli amanti: set to music by Mozart* (New York, 1819)

Memorie, ed. Cesare Pagnini (Milan, 1960)

Memorie – Libretti mozartiani (Milan, 1976)

Fekete de Galántha, János, *Wien im Jahre 1787: Skizze eines lebenden Bildes von Wien, entworfen von einem Weltbürger*, transl. from the French and ed. Victor Klarwill (Vienna, 1921)

Goldoni, Carlo, *Mémoires de M. Goldoni, pour servir à l'histoire de sa vie, et à celle de son théâtre* (1787), ed. Giuseppe Ortolani, in Goldoni, *Tutte le opere* (Milan, 2/1943)

Heinse, Friedrich, *Reise- und Lebens-Skizzen nebst dramaturgischen Blättern. 1. Teil* (Leipzig, 1837)

Hoffmann, E. T. A., 'Der Dichter und der Componist' (The poet and the composer, 1813), translated by Martyn Clarke, in *E. T. A. Hoffmann's musical writings: Kreisleriana, The poet and the composer, music criticism*, ed. David Charlton (Cambridge, 1989), pp. 188–209

Kelly, Michael, *Reminiscences of Michael Kelly, of the King's Theatre, and Theatre Royal Drury Lane, including a period of nearly half a century; with original anecdotes of many distinguished persons, political, literary, and musical*, 2 vols. (London, 1826)

Mozart: Briefe und Aufzeichnungen, ed. Wilhelm A. Bauer, Otto Erich Deutsch and Joseph Heinz Eibl, 7 vols. (Kassel, 1962–75)

195

Němetschek [Niemetschek], Franz Xaver, *Lebensbeschreibung des k. k. Kapellmeisters Wolfgang Amadeus Mozart, aus Originalquellen* (Prague, 2/1808; repr. Leipzig, 1978)

Nissen, Georg Nikolaus von, *Anhang zu W. A. Mozarts Biographie, nach Originalbriefen, Sammlungen alles über ihn Geschriebenen, mit vielen neuen Beylagen, Steindrücken, Musikblättern und einem Facsimile*, ed. Constanze Mozart Nissen (Leipzig, 1828; repr. Hildesheim, 1964)

Novello, Vincent and Mary, *A Mozart pilgrimage. Being the travel diaries of Vincent & Mary Novello in the year 1829*, ed. Rosemary Hughes (London, 1955)

Pezzl, Johann, *Skizze von Wien [1786-1790]. Ein Kultur- und Sittenbild aus der josefinischen Zeit*, ed. Gustav Gugitz and Anton Schlossar (Graz, 1923)

Rellstab, Ludwig, *Aus meinem Leben*, 2 vols. (Berlin, 1861)

Rochlitz, Friedrich, '*Nachschrift* zur Recension von *Eyblers Requiem*', *Allgemeine musikalische Zeitung*, 28:21 (24 May 1826), col. 337-40

'Noch einige Kleinigkeiten aus Mozarts Leben', *Allgemeine musikalische Zeitung* 3:35 (27 May 1801), col. 590-6

Ulybyshev, Aleksandr, *Nouvelle Biographie de Mozart, suivie. . .de l'analyse des principales œuvres de Mozart*, 3 vols. (Moscow, 1843)

Secondary sources

Abert, Hermann, *W. A. Mozart. . .Neubearbeitete und erweiterte Ausgabe von Otto Jahns Mozart, Zweiter Teil (1783-1791)*, 6th edn. (Leipzig, 1924)

Ackermann, Peter, 'Zwischen Kritik und Provokation: *Così fan tutte* in den Programmheften', in Vill, ed., *Beiträge*, 175-82

Angermüller, Rudolph, 'Bemerkungen zu französischen Bearbeitungen des 19. Jahrhunderts', in Vill, ed., *Beiträge*, 67-90

'Weigl, Joseph (ii)', *The New Grove*, 20:296-8

Mozart's operas, transl. Stewart Spencer (New York, 1988)

Brandstetter, Gabriele, 'So machen's alle: Die frühen Übersetzungen von Da Pontes und Mozarts "Così fan tutte" für deutsche Bühnen', *Musikforschung*, 35:1 (January-March 1982), 27-44

Carter, Tim, 'Ariosto, Ludovico', *The New Grove dictionary of opera*, ed. Stanley Sadie, 4 vols. (London, 1992), 1:191-2

W. A. Mozart: Le nozze di Figaro (Cambridge, 1987; Cambridge Opera Handbooks)

Csampai, Attila, and Dietmar Holland, eds., *Wolfgang Amadeus Mozart, Così fan tutte: Texte, Materialien, Kommentare* (Hamburg, 1984)

Darnton, Robert, *Mesmerism and the end of the Enlightenment in France* (Cambridge, Mass., 1968)

Dent, Edward J., *Mozart's operas: A critical study* (London, Oxford, New York, 2/1947)

Deutsch, Otto Erich, compiled and ed., *Mozart: Die Dokumente seines Lebens* (Kassel, 1961)

Dietrich, Margret, 'Dokumentation zur Uraufführung', in Vill, ed., *Beiträge*, pp. 24-53

Dunstan, Elizabeth M., 'Da Ponte and Ariosto' (unpublished typescript)

Edge, Dexter, 'Mozart's fee for *Così fan tutte*', *Journal of the Royal Musical Association*, 116:2 (November 1991), 211–35

'Mozart's reception in Vienna, 1787–1791', in *Wolfgang Amadè Mozart: Essays on his life and his music* (Oxford University Press; in press)

Einstein, Alfred, *Mozart: His character, his work*, transl. Arthur Mendel and Nathan Broder (Oxford, 1945)

Finscher, Ludwig, 'Mozarts "musikalische Regie": eine musikdramaturgische Analyse', in Vill, ed., *Beiträge*, pp. 9–23

Ford, Charles, *Così? Sexual politics in Mozart's operas* (Manchester, 1991)

Gallarati, Paolo, 'Music and masks in Lorenzo Da Ponte's Mozartian librettos', *Cambridge opera journal*, 1:3 (November 1989), 225–47

Gidwitz, Patricia Lewy, 'Vocal profiles of four Mozart sopranos' (Ph.D. thesis, Univ. of California, Berkeley, 1991)

and John A. Rice, 'Ferrarese, Adriana', *The New Grove dictionary of opera*, 2:162

Glöckner, Hans-Peter, 'Die Popularisierung der Unmoral: *Così fan tutte* in der Belletristik', in Vill, ed., *Beiträge*, pp. 112–26

Goldin, Daniela, 'Aspetti della librettistica italiana fra 1770 e 1830', *Analecta musicologica*, 21 (1982), 128–91

'Da Ponte librettista fra Goldoni e Casti', *Giornale storico della letteratura italiana*, 158 (1981), 396–408

La vera fenice: Librettisti e libretti tra Sette e Ottocento (Turin, 1985)

Golubev, Viktor, *Marivaux' Lustspiele in deutschen Übersetzungen des 18. Jahrhunderts* (Heidelberg, 1904)

Gombrich, Ernst, '*Così fan tutte* (Procris included)', *Journal of the Warburg and Courtauld Institutes*, 17 (1954), 372–4

Gugitz, Gustav, and Emil Karl Blümml, *Von Leuten und Zeiten im alten Wien* (Vienna and Leipzig, 1922)

Hanslick, Eduard, *Die moderne Oper: Kritiken und Studien* (Berlin, 1875); on *Così*: pp. 43–7; reprinted in Csampai and Holland, eds., *Così fan tutte: Texte, Materialien, Kommentare*, pp. 228–32

Heartz, Daniel, *Mozart's operas*, ed., with contributing essays, by Thomas Bauman (Berkeley and Los Angeles, 1990)

Hocquard, Jean-Victor, *Così fan tutte* (Paris, 1978)

Hodges, Sheila, *Lorenzo da Ponte: The life and times of Mozart's librettist* (New York, 1985)

Hortschansky, Klaus, 'Gegen Unwahrscheinlichkeit und Frivolität: die Bearbeitungen im 19. Jahrhundert', in Vill, ed., *Beiträge*, pp. 54–66

Hunter, Mary, '*Così fan tutte* et les conventions musicales de son temps', *L'avant-scène Opéra: Così fan tutte*, no. 131–2 (May–June 1990), 158–64

'Some representations of *opera seria* in *opera buffa*', *Cambridge opera journal*, 3:2 (July 1991), 89–108

Keller, Hans, 'Mozart's wrong key signature', *Tempo*, n. 98 (1972), 21–7

Köhler, Karl-Heinz, 'Die Rezeption der Mozart-Opern unter Goethes Theaterleitung im Jahrzehnt nach dem Tode des Komponisten: Ein Beitrag zur Wirkungsgeschichte des Mozartschen Schaffens im Spiegel der Weimarer Klassik', *Mozart-Jahrbuch* 1991 (Bericht über den Internationalen Mozart-Kongreß Salzburg 1991; Kassel, 1992), 231–6

Kramer, Kurt, 'Da Pontes "Così fan tutte"', *Nachrichten der Akademie der Wissenschaften in Göttingen* (1. Philologisch-historische Klasse, Jhrg. 1973, no. 1; Göttingen, 1973), 1–27

Kritsch, Cornelia, and Herbert Zeman, 'Das Rätsel eines genialen Opernentwurfs – Da Pontes Libretto zu "Così fan tutte" und das literarische Umfeld des 18. Jahrhunderts', in *Die österreichische Literatur: Ihr Profil an der Wende vom 18. zum 19. Jahrhundert (1750–1830)* (Graz, 1979), 355–76

Kunze, Stefan, *Mozarts Opern* (Stuttgart, 1984)

'Schein und Sein in Mozarts Ouvertüre zu *«Così fan tutte»*', *Schweizer Jahrbuch für Musikwissenschaft*, Neue Folge 3 (1983), 65–78

'Über das Verhältnis von musikalisch autonomer Struktur und Textbau in Mozarts Opern: Das Terzettino "Soave sia il vento" (Nr. 10) aus Così fan tutte"', *Mozart-Jahrbuch* 1973/4, 217–32

Landon, H. C. Robbins, *Mozart and Vienna* (London and New York, 1991)

Mozart: The golden years (London and New York, 1989)

Link, Dorothea, '"Così fan tutte": Dorabella and Amore', *Mozart-Jahrbuch* 1991, 888–94

'The Viennese operatic canon and Mozart's *Così fan tutte*', *Mitteilungen der Internationalen Stiftung Mozarteum*, 38 (1990), 111–21

Littlejohn, David, 'Reflections on Peter Sellars's Mozart', *Opera quarterly*, 7:2 (Summer 1990), 6–36

Michtner, Otto, *Das alte Burgtheater als Opernbühne von der Einführung des deutschen Singspiels (1778) bis zum Tod Kaiser Leopolds II. (1792)* (Theatergeschichte Österreichs, 3:1; Graz, Vienna, Cologne, 1970)

Miller, Jonathan, *Subsequent performances* (New York, 1986)

Mozart, Wolfgang Amadeus, *Così fan tutte*, in Mozart, *Neue Ausgabe sämtlicher Werke*, ed. Linda Faye Ferguson and Wolfgang Rehm, II/5:xviii (Kassel, 1991)

Noiray, Michel, 'Commentaire musical et littéraire', *L'avant-scène Opéra: Così fan tutte*, 131–2 (May-June 1990), 39–144

Noske, Frits, 'Così fan tutte: Dramatic irony', in *The signifier and the signified: Studies in the operas of Mozart and Verdi* (The Hague, 1977), pp. 93–120

Payer von Thurn, Rudolf, *Joseph II. als Theaterdirektor* (Vienna and Leipzig, 1920)

Platoff, John, 'Musical and dramatic structure in the *opera buffa* finale', *Journal of musicology*, 7 (1989), 191–230

Prod'homme, Gabriel, '*Così fan tutte* de Mozart et ses transformations depuis 1790', *Le ménestrel*, 87 (1925), 265–7, 277–80.

Puntscher Riekmann, Sonja, '"Così fan tutte": Die Lehre der Gefühlsrelativität', in *Mozart: ein bürgerlicher Künstler. Studien zu den Libretti 'Le nozze di Figaro', 'Don Giovanni', und 'Così fan tutte'* (Junge Wiener Romanistik 4; Vienna, Cologne and Graz, 1982)

Raeburn, Christopher, 'Bussani, Francesco', *The New Grove*, 3:512

Rice, John A., 'Emperor and impresario: Leopold II and the transformation of Viennese musical theater, 1790–1792', Ph.D. thesis (Univ. of California, Berkeley, 1987)

'Rondò vocali di Salieri e Mozart per Adriana Ferrarese', *I vicini di Mozart*, ed. Maria Teresa Muraro and David Bryant (Florence, 1989), 185–209

'Scuola de' gelosi, La', *The New Grove dictionary of opera*, 4:278

W. A. Mozart: *La clemenza di Tito* (Cambridge, 1991; Cambridge Opera Handbooks)

Rosen, Charles, *The classical style* (New York, 1971)

Rüdiger, Horst, 'Die Abenteuer des Lorenzo da Ponte', in *Die Österreichische Literatur: Ihr Profil an der Wende vom 18. zum 19. Jahrhundert (1750–1830)* (Graz, 1979), pp. 331–53

Rushton, Julian, '*Così fan tutte*', *The New Grove dictionary of opera*, 1:965–8

Schindler, Otto, 'Das Publikum des Burgtheaters in der Josephinischen Ära', in Margaret Dietrich, ed., *Das Burgtheater und sein Publikum*, 1 (Vienna, 1976), pp. 11–95

Schuler, Manfred, 'Eine Prager Singspielfassung von Mozarts "Così fan tutte" aus der Zeit des Komponisten', *Mozart-Jahrbuch* 1991, 895–901

Sheffield, Graham, '*Così fan tutte*' (pp. 86–105), *Opera on record*, ed. Alan Blyth (discographies compiled by Malcolm Walker; London, 1979)

Splitt, Gerhard, 'Gespielte Aufklärung: *Così fan tutte* oder die Umkehrung der Moral', in *Freiburger Universitätsblätter*, 101 (September 1988: *Mozart oder die Physiognomie des Schöpferischen*), 47–71

Starobinski, Jean, 'Tromper pour détromper', in programme book for *Così fan tutte*, Théâtre du Châtelet (Paris, 1992), 24–9

Steptoe, Andrew, *The Mozart–Da Ponte operas: The cultural and musical background to Le nozze di Figaro, Don Giovanni, and Così fan tutte* (Oxford, 1988)

'The sources of *Così fan tutte*: A reappraisal', *Music and letters*, 62 (1981), 281–94

Stone, John, 'The background to the libretto', in *Così fan tutte* (English National Opera Guide no. 22; London and New York, 1983), 33–45

Strauss, Richard, 'Mozarts *Così fan tutte*' (1910); quoted in Csampai and Holland, eds., *Così fan tutte: Texte, Materialien, Kommentare*, pp. 233–9

Strohm, Reinhard, *Italienische Opernarien des frühen Settecento (1720–1730)* (*Analecta musicologica*, 16:1–2; Cologne, 1976)

Till, Nicholas, *Mozart and the Enlightenment: Truth, virtue and beauty in Mozart's operas* (London and Boston, 1991)

Tovey, Donald Francis, 'The Overture to "Così fan tutte"', in *Essays in musical analysis* (Oxford, 1935–9), 6:30–1

Tyson, Alan, *Mozart: Studies of the autograph scores* (Cambridge, Mass. and London, 1987)

'Notes on the composition of Mozart's *Così fan tutte*', *Journal of the American Musicological Society*, 37:2 (Summer 1984), 356–401

Vill, Susanne, ed., *Così fan tutte: Beiträge zur Wirkungsgeschichte von Mozarts Oper* (Schriften zum Musiktheater, 2; Bayreuth, 1978)

Wagner, Richard, *Oper und Drama* (1851), in *Richard Wagner's prose works*, transl. William Ashton Ellis, 8 vols. (London, 1892–9; repr. New York, 1966)

Webster, James, 'The analysis of Mozart's arias', in Cliff Eisen, ed., *Mozart studies* (Oxford, 1991), pp. 101–99

Werner-Jensen, Karin, '*Così fan tutte* im Angebot der Musikverleger', in Vill, ed., *Beiträge*, pp. 99–111

Williams, Bernard, 'Passion and cynicism: Remarks on *Così fan tutte*', *The musical times*, 114:1562 (April 1973), 361–4

Wollzogen, Alexander von, 'Mozart's *Così fan tutte* auf der deutschen Bühne', *Deutsche Musik-Zeitung*, 2 (1861), 137–40, 145–8, 241–4, 249–54

Zietsch, Heinz, 'Die Berichterstattung in den Musikzeitschriften und Tageszeitungen des 19. Jahrhunderts', in Vill, ed., *Beiträge*, pp. 132–47

Index

opera buffa,
conventions 2, 42, 54, 57–8, 70, 80,
95, 100, 108, 110, 135, 137,
139–41, 157, 189 n. 12
finales, 33, 77, 146, 147, 150, 154;
see also Così fan tutte, Nos. 18,
31
parody 17–18, 190 n. 23
opera seria,
conventions and parody, 17–18, 30,
35, 38, 39, 42, 43, 44, 46, 47, 51,
60, 100, 101, 108, 122, 125,
127–30, 132–3, 147
Orlando furioso, see Ariosto
Orsini-Rosenberg, Franz, see
Rosenberg, Franz Graf Orsini-
Osthoff, Wolfgang, 187 n. 22
Östman, Arnold, 181
Ovid (Publius Ovidius Naso),
Metamorphoses, 59–60

Paisiello, Giovanni,
Il barbiere di Siviglia, 6–7, 137, 183
n. 12
I filosofi immaginari, 84
Il re Teodoro in Venezia, 79, 161
Palissot de Montenoy, Charles, *Les
Philosophes*, 83
Paris, 9, 70, 166, 171, 176, 180
pastoral literature, 86
Payer von Thurn, Rudolf, 191 n. 7
Perinet, Joachim, *Der theatralischer
Guckkasten*, 93–4
Petrarch (Francesco Petrarca), 58, 62,
69, 130, 190 n. 27
Petrosellini, Giuseppe, 6, 79
Pezzl, Johann, 16;
*Faustin oder Das aufgeklärte
philosophische Jahrhundert*, 87,
188 n. 10
Skizze von Wien, 86–9, 90, 92
philosophy, *see Così fan tutte*,
philosophy in
Platoff, John, 147
Pohl, Carl Friedrich, 160
Ponnelle, Jean-Pierre, 176
Porter, Andrew, 192 n. 33
Prager Theater-Almanach, 48
Prague, 9, 15, 164, 165, 167, 171
Pritchard, Sir John, 175
proverbs, *see Così fan tutte*, libretto,
proverbs
Puchberg, Michael, 1, 8, 19, 23, 24
Purchase, New York, 177–8

quotation, *see Così fan tutte* (K588),
quotation

Raeburn, Christopher, 192 n. 20
Rameau, Jean-Phillipe, *Les Indes
galantes*, 86
Rehm, Wolfgang, 189 n. 3, 192 n. 19
Rellstab, Ludwig, 170, 193 n. 47
Rice, John A., 10, 160, 184 n. 9, 187
nn. 31, 42, 191 nn. 4, 5, 11, 192
nn. 16, 28
Richelet, Pierre, *Dictionnaire* (rev.
Wailly), 84, 188 n. 4
Rochlitz, Friedrich, 7, 116–17, 125,
136, 155, 169, 171, 185 n. 34,
194 n. 53
Romani, Felice, *Il turco in Italia*, 166
Roocroft, Amanda, 180
Rosen, Charles, 70–1
Rosenberg, Franz Graf Orsini-, (1), 8
Rossini, Giocchino, 108;
Il turco in Italia, 166
Rousseau, Jean-Jacques,
Le Devin du village, 79
Émile, ou De l'éducation, 85
Rushton, Julian, 188 n. 16

Sade, Donatien, Marquis de, 86;
La Philosophie dans le boudoir, 84
Salieri, Antonio, 19, 24, 160;
and Da Ponte, 10–11, 14, 20
Axur, re d'Ormus, 9, 58, 69, 75
La cifra, 160
La grotta di Trofonio, 11, 65–6,
78–9, 95
Prima la musica e poi le parole, 69,
77
La scola degli amanti (aborted
version of *Così fan tutte*), 10–11,
12–13, 20, 81, 184 nn. 9, 13
La scuola de' gelosi, 79
Sannazaro, Jacopo, *L'Arcadia*, 14, 32,
69–70, 111, 125, 137
Sarti, Giuseppe, *Fra i due litiganti il
terzo gode*, 191 n. 1
Schaaf, Johannes, 177
Scheidemantel, Carl, *Die Dame Kobold*,
173
Schikaneder, Emanuele, 2
Schmidt, Johann Friedrich, *Wer ist in
der Liebe unbeständig?*, 71
Schmieder, Heinrich Gottlieb, 168
Schott (music publishers), 170
Schröder, Friedrich Ludwig, *Liebe und
Versuchung*, 168